Dramatic Play
in Childhood

Dramatic Play in Childhood

Rehearsal for Life

V. Glasgow Koste
Illustrations by Susan Russell
Foreword by Holly N. Giffin

Heinemann
Portsmouth, NH

Heinemann
A division of Reed Elsevier Inc.
361 Hanover Street
Portsmouth, NH 03801-3912

Offices and agents throughout the world

We would like to thank those who have given their permission to include material in this book. Every effort has been made to contact the copyright holders for permission to reprint borrowed material where necessary. We regret any oversights that may have occurred and would be happy to rectify them in future printings of this work.

Excerpt from "Send in the Clowns" by Stephen Sondheim. Copyright 1973 Revelation Music Publishing Corp. and Rilting Music, Inc. A Tommy Valando Publication. Reprinted by permission of the publisher.

Library of Congress Cataloging-in-Publication Data
Koste, Virginia Glasgow.
    Dramatic play in childhood: rehearsal for life/Virginia Glasgow Koste; illustrations by Susan Russell: foreword by Holly N. Giffin.
        p. cm.
    Includes bibliographical references.
    ISBN 0-435-08669-3 (alk. paper)
    1. Play—Psychological aspects. 2. Drama—Psychological aspects.
3. Child psychology. I. Title.
    BF717.K67 1995
    155.4'18—dc20

Editor: Lisa Barnett
Cover design: Julie Hahn

Printed in the United States of America on acid-free paper

98 97 96 95   EB   1 2 3 4 5 6

For all my children

Contents

Acknowledgments

The accumulated wisdom and experience of countless contributors have gone into the making of this book. The collaboration of student and teacher is a strong bond; we teach one another, we learn together. So my gratitude to all of my teachers and to all of my students is herewith acknowledged. Of these, the ones whose writing is quoted, and to whom very special appreciation must be expressed, include:

Christy Anspach, Gayle Armstrong, Evelyn Avsharian, Marguerite Beavers, Paula Blok, Beverly Brennan, Carol Brooks, Barbara Ann Brown, Cheryl Brown, Annis Calhoun, Kay Carroll, Robin Casarjian, Bonita Casey, Marcia Coakley, Carolyn J. Cogdill, Thelma Coleman, Marjorie Coplas, Kay Cosma, Sandra Dodd, Jill Donnellan, Gloria K. Downing, Pauline M. Dugan, H.V. Emsbe, Tom Fahlstrom, Jessie Florence, Donna Ford, Janet Forster, Pat Freeman, Penelope Frostic, Janet Goebel, Nancy Gould, Gloria Gregory, Debie Guthrie, Ruth Hartley, Marilyn Hazlett, Linda Heidenreich, Sharron Henson, Gail Hering, Donna Marie James, Pat Jenzen, Donelda Johnston, Carol Sue Jones, Sue Kime, Sharon Klenk, Mary Klos, Jane Kolarik, Janis LaRue, Ruth Lee, Janet Livingstone, Elizabeth Loy, Janet Lucas, Barbara Ann Lucier, Alexandria Madias, Ruth Martin, Harry Matrone, Pat McDonald, Ann McGuire, Lois Moore, Karen Moscow, Suzanne Mull, Holly Neal, Cynthia Nichols, Marg E. Noone, Lynn Parsons, Rita Paye, Elaine L. Pero, G. Phillips, Donald Ragland, Sally Ramsey, Beverly Schroeder, Mattie Shepherd, Kathy Sinclair, John Skinner, Virginia Spooner, Diana Sprague, Lorene Stader, Judith Stanlake, Ruth Steinki, Maureen Strang, Edinna Taylor, Lana Traub, Donavee Vigus, E. Voltzikos, Gretchen Voyle, Mary Warner, Karen Weaver, Vicki Weinberg, Jeanne Weinch, Carol Welty, Ruth Wert, Ruth Ann Wescott, Pat Wesley, and Virginia Williams.

My love and thanks go also to "editors-in-residence" Walt, Tory, and Pamela; to colleague-in-play/work Thelma McDaniel; and to editors Orlin Corey and Lisa Barnett, for their manifest faith in the importance of what this book tries to say.

Foreword

In the summer of 1969, as a college student on vacation, I followed a friend of mine into a class taught at a local university. There I encountered a remarkable teacher named Virginia Koste, and the remarkable idea that the transformational power of dramatic play is essentially linked to learning, creating, and being human. I left that first class with a bounce in my step and a lightness in my heart. I returned every day—an illicit learner—for once not compelled by grades or graduation but by an inner thirst to know more.

Years later when I first read Jinny Koste's book *Dramatic Play in Childhood: Rehearsal for Life*, I thought "This is just like being in her class!" Here was the same joyous, playful mixture of authoritative sources, from the two-year-old child to the two-thousand-year-old philosopher, interlaced with her own penetrating insights. The message is and was the same: Child's play is the natural source of mature creative thinking and expression, the birthright of humans everywhere.

The form of the book as well as the content captures the spirit of her teaching and the spirit of play itself. Like play, this research does not attempt to wrest "right answers" from the data but rather pursues possibilities. Each chapter provides a new lens through which to look at play and no lens claims to show all there is to see. Indeed, the tyranny of the "one right answer" would kill a study of play as surely as it kills play itself.

Koste demonstrates what the play process looks like from the player's point of view: from imitation to transformation, flowing in and out of time, in and out of realities. She illustrates the complexity and sophistication of the player's skills and purposes in constructing make-believe worlds. Indeed, her approach has influenced the method and focus of developmental research on social pretend play over the past decade.

Koste's steadfast emphasis on learning to "see with one's own eyes" is the basis for her authentic understanding of play, her effectiveness as a teacher, and her rigorous approach to research. Students were asked to encounter play directly, like players, learning what it is to them, without benefit of a prescribed "right way" to see. Student voices are rendered faithfully. Stories are left intact. Thus, the reader, too, is given as direct contact with the data as possible.

At the time of this latest printing, much has changed in the world. And yet some essential struggles are still at issue. In the field of education there is tension between the growing concern that children meet external, culturally-approved standards, and the growing body of research and theory suggesting that learning is far more complex and individuated than the standard-makers ever thought.

Recent research suggests that teaching that strives primarily to train young people to meet traditional standards is inadequate. It often focuses on only a small part of the total spectrum of human intelligences. It often presents content in ways that speak only to certain modes of accessing information and only certain styles of making information meaningful. This approach rewards only those who learn and produce in traditionally prescribed and valued ways.

Many children who learn different things in different ways sacrifice their natural talent in order to conform. Others, unable to squeeze into the mold, are inevitably emotionally damaged and may drop out entirely. As a society hurtling through changes at an ever-accelerating rate, depending upon abilities that have not yet been anticipated to solve problems that have not yet been named, we cannot afford to waste our children's talent and intelligence.

In transformational play, Koste presents us with a natural pedagogy that honors the individual experience and celebrates a multitude of possible ways of questing and knowing. She makes an impassioned plea for protecting and preserving the child's essential freedom in play. This is the freedom to be directed by inner callings rather than external expectations. It is the freedom to wonder, to experiment, to invent. It is a freedom that, if allowed to flourish, fuels the creative fires of adulthood.

She gives evidence time and again that, rather than generating chaos, the impulse of the child in free, natural play is to discover order and to create new orders when old ones no longer suffice. She lovingly uncovers the internal logic that guides the player.

Inevitably, the creations of play delight us as adults. They give us a fresh perspective on our realities. They inspire us to recapture and reclaim our own original creative powers in living our own lives.

This seminal study, reflecting a lifetime of teaching and thinking, presents a grounded argument to educators, researchers, parents, scientists, and artists, for renewing our faith in the human impulse to learn and to create. It commands respect for play, in all its forms, as a basic mode of human inquiry. *Dramatic Play in Childhood: Rehearsal for Life* takes the reader on an exhilarating rollercoaster ride through the possibilities generated by the transformational imagination, touching down in the real play of real children, soaring to visions of our human potential, brimming with creativity, power, and hope.

Holly N. Giffin, Ph.D.
Director, Mt. Altos Institute
for the Study of Human Communication
and Development
Research Committee
American Alliance for Theatre and Education

Introduction

In this little book Jinny Koste plunges you immediately into the world of children's drama. You are indeed initiated into the open secrets of play!

It is little wonder that Jinny Koste would use a writing style that plunges you into children's drama. It is Jinny Koste! She has herself been immersed in the world of drama and theatre all of her life. Artfully she uses this intimate picture of the drama of children to show how they grow and learn through play. This book also provides an intimate immersion into children's thinking and creative problem solving.

Although you may stand in awe of the tremendous skill of Jinny Koste in using drama to facilitate learning, thinking, and problem solving, somehow the feeling is communicated that "you too can do it." The communication is so intimate that you really feel that you have been initiated into the open secrets of children's play. You feel that you have the "key."

At the very outset of the book you get the feeling that here is someone who understands adult, real-life creativity and who knows how to elicit creative thinking from children. Jinny Koste acknowledges that creativity goes beyond the rational, logical, sequential processing of information. The intimate descriptions of children's drama make this acknowledgment concrete. They show how it actually happens.

In this book, Jinny Koste does not waste time in trying to define "creativity," "play," or "drama." She simply goes ahead and artfully describes the intimate manifestations of creativity, play, and drama. She accomplishes this so expertly that you "know" what "creativity," "play," and "drama" are. You might not be able to transform this "knowing" into words. But you "know."

The descriptions of children's dramatic behavior are full of examples of both conscious and unconscious behavior. You can experience them through the vivid images of Jinny Koste's descriptions. You become convinced that play really is a powerful way to learn.

As you read this book, be prepared to raise your consciousness of the thinking of children and to deepen your understanding of the art of play.

E. Paul Torrance
Department of Educational Psychology
The University of Georgia
Athens, Georgia

For the last five years or so, it has become possible to speak about aesthetic development as if it were a tangible event—subject to measurement, and maybe even to manipulation (a bad word, manipulation, but all education certainly assumes its presence). Even at fashionable cocktail parties, or in the pages of the *New York Times*, one can mention this term—"aesthetic development"—and have some hopes of being understood. After all, the child develops physically, emotionally, intellectually, etc.; and we can talk about development in each of these areas. Surely, by talking about aesthetic development we confirm the fact that the child develops aesthetically, too. The catch is that nobody has yet come up with a good enough operational definition of aesthetic development to make it as visible to the researcher as a tape measure makes physical development, or a good test makes intellectual development. It isn't "development" that is so hard to visualize; it is "aesthetic."

In this book, when Jinny Koste talks about *play* and *transformation*, I think she is uncovering the tangible roots of the aesthetic development of mankind. Basically, aesthetics is the ability to treat the "as if;" to react in a sensory and emotional way to conventionalized stimuli; to see the waterfall instead of the pigment; to empathize with Willy Loman instead of merely watching an actor speak memorized lines. This ability to pretend is called "art" in adult life, but "play" in childhood—that early stage of our lives when we are not yet grown too lazy or inhibited to do our own makebelieving. This book paints childhood as not only that stage when we are rehearsing for life; but also the time when we are living for the joy of the rehearsal.

Many books have been written about play; and many about art; but rarely has a book about play so clearly revealed the basic development of art.

Moses Goldberg
Artistic Director
Stage One: Louisville Children's Theatre

All young children can be observed rehearsing for life through dramatic play. Few adults can be observed in the same process. Yet the impulse which helps us learn so much when we are young remains with us throughout our lives. Each of us can probably remember a recent moment when we rehearsed in our imaginations a future event where the outcome was uncertain. Perhaps it was an annual evaluation session with our supervisor, or a job interview, or perhaps a confrontation with a family member. Some of us rehearse the dialogue only, repeating ways to say something and listening to expected responses. Others go through an entire imaginary dress rehearsal with costumes (should I appear staid or carefree?) and settings (should we meet in the office or over lunch?). Indeed, I wonder if we ever stop rehearsing for these moments.

The dramatic impulse to act out future uncertainties appears to be common to all of us. Virginia Koste penetrates beneath the surface of this process in its most primitive form, with the young child, to reveal what is really happening underneath. The result will enlighten many. Her analysis will help teachers and parents recognize the meaning and form of dramatic play, the known from which they can guide children to explore unknown worlds. Serious theatre students will gain insights into the process of role taking as they study the very young dramatic artist trying to achieve the goal of all artists—to order, clarify, and understand human experience.

The author brings us her revelations about children in dramatic play with the eyes and ears of an experienced educator as well as an accomplished theatre artist. Thus, we finally have a book about dramatic play written by one who thoroughly understands theatre and drama. This in itself makes the book a unique and welcome addition to our literature.

Judith Baker Kase
The University of South Florida
Tampa, Florida

1978:
Backstage
of this Book

The hope and thrust of this book is to *describe the art of dramatic play in childhood through its manifestations*—which is, after all, the basic mode of most of art and science. So, playing with that idea, I set to work.

Looking back on my own childhood, I can see that being cradled in a wardrobe trunk marked THEATRE: RUSH and raised by actor-parents in hotels and dressing-rooms could have been expected to nurture a nature immersed in playing/Playing. At a time when I was still busily playing dress-up in my mother's costumes, someone named Corinne Brown (in the Teacher Training Department of the Ethical Culture School in New York City) was already writing a book modestly called *Creative Drama in the Lower School*, the first chapter of which was to be entitled "Dramatic Play" and was to state: "Drama is dramatic play grown up. . ."

The arts of drama and theatre are rooted in the natural dramatic playing of childhood. Essentially, they are separated only by degree points along the same continuum. The theatre experience is a heightened kind of playing—developed, externalized, and shaped by seasoned and trained talent and life-knowledge into audible and visible form so that it is worthy of being purposefully given by artists to those other theatre-eventful participants we call audience: the "seers" for whom "the seeing place" exists.

Along that flowing continuum, the cardboard boxes and torn curtains of child's play develop into the stage visions of an Appia; the cast-off dress-ups of our earliest disguises meld into the costumes of a Tanya Moiseiwitsch; primitive hums and chants and tin-pan drumming fuse into a Bernstein score; the torso-twist of poison tag turns into Balanchine choreography; "I'm the King of the Mountain" rises into *Oedipus Rex*. *Child's play, charged with suspense and conflict, is rooted in imitation and centered in transformation: the essential elements of drama/theatre.*

And along the middle of the continuum, at the center and radiating in a galaxy of myriad directions, are those extensions and elaborations of child's play which we name improvisation, creative drama, and sociodrama. This central realm of experiential, exploratory drama work/play is rich with barely-tried potential uses (from education to social work, from police training to rehabilitation, from therapy to self-realization) for all ages and conditions of human beings.

So it is my early-seeded and long-growing conviction that anyone working in any phase of drama, theatre, communications, or education needs to draw upon the natural resource that is child's play. Effectual practitioners do in fact use their powers of play—spontaneously, unconsciously—in their work. Most of them probably even realize that they do. But now the time is upon us to validate and expand our knowledge of this intricate process, in order to keep the continuum flowing from the child's explorings on into optimal maturity of achievement and being. In theatre, true improvising follows the rhythms and motives of the child at play; so do real rehearsing, designing and acting.

So, furthermore, does genuine teaching and learning and trying and making of any kind. The world *is* a stage (a place to play with all of the possibilities), and the men and women in it—like the children—are players. . . but not "merely." If child's play does indeed contain the seeds of mature creative work, then the dramatic imagination may be a natural power of more pervasive significance than has yet been realized.

Maybe we were all born in that moveable, magical trunk, and—like the wondrous wardrobe that gives into Narnia for those with the vision and insight to see fathomless worlds—it may always be open, running over with transformable stuff that turns into, turns out to be treasure.

—Jinny Koste

1995:
Looking Again
(A Scattering of
Thoughts)

This book—first published in 1978—was written in 1976; labor was induced by such signs as a terse note from a beloved former student: "Where is your book? We *need* it."

Sometimes it's true that the more things change, the more they stay the same. What this book said then, it still says now: since the natural power of *play* is essential to survival, we must recognize and nurture it in our children and in ourselves. And it still says it *play-fully* and seriously, through the evidence of real-life dialogue and action.

It is also true that the more things stay the same, the more they change. What has changed from then to now is the magnified *need* that the book serves. The world's degree of need has increased with emergency-room urgency, charged with the hope of saving lives at risk. Our children's. Our own.

To meet the need, we must *see* the need—that fact stays the same. We must see the need to recognize the importance of the ordinary in human growth of individuals of all ages. The native urge to play that makes babies drop things from high-chairs can engage instead of madden adults as long as we see and join the bonding joy of the child's testing of the theory of gravity. Like Albert Overhauser, who discovered dynamic nuclear polarization one afternoon in the lab while "playing around" with ideas which, once transformed to practical use, now save lives daily. Like Einstein's "vague play" in "searching for connections."

Now and always, among the practicing experts, there are the children, stretching their powers, playing, as well as all of the adults who have kept or revived those early powers, to flow into their ways of making a living, making a life, helping the world to keep turning.

During the years from the seventies to the nineties, a change to celebrate has been the expanding body of books and articles exploring the processes and purposes of play, such as psychologist Erik Erikson's masterful *Toys and Reasons*.

Another change strikes me as particularly relevant to this book's focus on *dramatic* play as generic. That change is the wide-spread absorption of drama/theatre metaphors into today's language. Not only such long-time usages as *curtains* and *theatre of war*, but a saturation of real life *scenarios*, of *staging* protests, of *playing roles*, of who/what is *waiting in the wings. A hard act to follow* and *cut to the chase* pepper the prose describing and predicting what may next be *scripted* into history.

"Maybe theatre is. . . a condensed version of all the imagined, depicted, and theorized spheres. . . by which we attempt coherencies. . . in the complexity. . . of existence." It was not a playwright or an actor or a drama teacher who said that, but Erikson.

With awareness growing as our need grows, now may be the time for a broader understanding of dramatic play as a microcosm of life itself. To see, with Johan Huizinga, that "genuine, pure play *is* one of the main bases of civilization."

I still believe my premise that "dramatic imagination may be a natural power of more pervasive significance than has yet been realized." Maybe in time, the evidence will be acknowledged and acted on widely enough for a re-write: "may be" may be transformed into "is."

Meanwhile, may the pages that follow call up what you already knew before you could read, what you've grown to know since then— and, as you keep on searching—what comes next.

—V. Glasgow Koste (a.k.a. Jinny)

*Dramatic Play
in Childhood*

"Understanding the atom bomb is child's play, compared with understanding child's play."

London Times liner

CHAPTER ONE

Play Is the Thing

Play is the thing
    —wherein we'll catch the conscious and unconscious of humankind.

". . . the great instinctive forces of civilized life . . . law and order, commerce and profit, craft and art, poetry, wisdom, and science. All are rooted in the primeval soil of play . . . genuine, pure play is one of the main bases of civilization."

Johan Huizinga

"We who have proved magnificently that any number can work are now compelled to prove that any number can play. . . . I plead for the play of the mind not on the ground that it is pleasant but on the ground that it is necessary."

Clifton Fadiman

"In Synectics theory, play with apparent irrelevancies is used extensively to generate energy for problem-solving and to evoke new viewpoints with respect to problems. . . . Play, as an attitude of mind and an ability on an adult level . . . operates in terms of the adult individual's willingness to recall and to re-enter the child state. . . . This plasticity of awareness and consciousness is characteristic of the child's approach to the world's multiplicity; thus, as in learning how to play, so in learning how to accept and use the irrelevant, the individual is involved in relearning, on an adult level, techniques which were "natural" in the intuitive vision of childhood . . . necessary to creativity on an adult level."

William J. J. Gordon, Cambridge Synectics group

"We ought surely to look in the child for the first traces of imaginative activity. The child's best loved and most absorbing occupation is play. Perhaps we may say that every child at play behaves like an imaginative writer, in that he creates a world of his own or, more truly he re-arranges the things of his world and orders it in a new way that pleases him better. . . . Language has preserved this relationship between children's play and poetic creation . . . 'plays'—'players.'"

Sigmund Freud

"A child's every experimental exercise is an invention . . . he reinvents post and lintel construction with his blocks . . . he makes a waterfall by detouring a rivulet. . . . Such acts reveal the inventive, form-making nature of the child's play."

W. J. J. Gordon

"Children are rich with all they do not own, rich with the potential wonders of their universe. Making believe is not only one of their earliest pleasures, it is their vital spark, the token of their liberty . . . "

Paul Hazard

Play, claims Von Lange, is the art of childhood, and art is the mature form of play. Paul Hazard pleads for the necessity to "respect the valor and eminent dignity of play." From Aristotle through Rousseau, to Freud, Piaget, Einstein, Bertrand Russell: the list of brilliant minds recognizing and studying play as the wellspring of human achievement, grows. In this century interest seems to be broadening and accelerating; Johan Huizinga's *Homo Ludens: A Study of The Play Element In Culture* (1944) is profoundly significant; an invaluable new contribution is *Play: Its Role In Development And Evolution* (1976), an anthology encompassing a range from Bruner, Groos, and Schiller, to Auden, Piaget, the Opies, Koestler, and Erikson.

Along with this learned attention to the phenomenon of play has come a veritable wave of popular notice, the quintessence of which is the cereal box-top—*Life* cereal, appropriately enough!—brought in to class by a student this very year, and bearing this text:

> This is one in a continuing series of a Learning Program designed to help you help your child.

ENCOURAGE YOUR CHILD TO PLAY

Playing is one of the most powerful ways for a child to learn. He looks at the world around him and plays what he sees—going to the office, driving a bus, make-believe stores or parties and on and on. He tries different ways of acting, assumes various roles and

challenges himself with all sorts of problems. And because it's only
playing, he can try out new things without fear of failure. Encourage
your child to play by providing him with opportunity, materials,
and adequate space. Treat yourself by watching him play. You
might even join once in awhile.

There is something quite stunning about the reduction of the ages' wisdom to an American box-top, which may have been read before long by
scores of millions (and sometimes read *to* the preliterates?) while eating breakfasts from California to Maine! Body and soul instantly fed.

But it is the wish and intent of this book to enter the realm of play in
another way. This book does not pretend to be scholarly or scientific—
others answer those needs abundantly and well; nor does it choose to
package capsulated advice—of which there is already a surfeit. Instead, a
stream of scenes—all real—follow, selected and arranged in the hope of
raising our consciousness and deepening our understanding of the art of
play. Marcel Marceau has said in an interview that he believes art must be
demonstrated rather than explained. Taking that precept a little further,
explanation may finally emerge only through demonstration; in both science and art, particulars embody abstractions.

For instance: the accumulated studies of scholars and scientists
verify that play is not a luxury; rather, a necessity for humankind. But
the following account* seems to me to illustrate that truth more memo-
rably than any expository statement alone ever could:

> This past week-end at a family reunion there were five boys
> between the ages of 4 and 2. While drinking punch, they watched all
> of the babies for a while and discussed why they were crying. They
> decided it was not because the babies were wet, or hungry or tired,
> but *because they couldn't play.*

That is an indelibly impressive statement of—and by—those children
on their own value system. It is by means of such documented scenes
that this book explores the form, content, and purposes of play. Thus
we can savor the best of both worlds, delighting in while drawing meaning from such evidence—rather like playing itself? No traditional text-
book is appropriate to so enchanting a subject.

It has already been pointed out, with the help of the great writers
enlisted at the outset, that play is fundamental, pervasive in its function-

---

*By a student in a child drama class at Eastern Michigan University.

ing throughout civilization and in all of the ages (both of history and of individual life-spans). This book focuses on *play in childhood* for three main reasons: that is the time when most people are most expert and constant in playing; that is the time when they most freely externalize their playing, so that it is possible to see and hear it; and that is the time when the power of play as a means of growth and accomplishment can most effectively be nurtured for a stronger rising generation of adults.

So it is *child's play* that we now concentrate on: specifically, dramatic play, by which I mean any play involving the mental act of imaginative *transformation.** Untermyer has called the child "the savage, the creator, and the god"; Stanislavski spoke of children as "the most high-minded, responsive, and ardent" in their reactions to life and to art. The child is naturally curious, intuitive, inclined to take risks, a spendthrift of energy, a joker, a maker, a seeker, and a finder. It is not sentimental to view childhood as an intense, open-questing condition; explosive, even dangerous in potential (Sylvia Ashton-Warner compares children to volcanoes). New to life, full of life, embracing life, open to all possibilities and impossibilities.

> 6-year-old Dawn said to me, "I think I will write a book." I said, "Oh? And what will you write about?" She replied, "About myself; so many things happen to me every day, I'm afraid I'll forget all these things if I don't write them down."

Maggie (9 years old):   I did my report on the beginnings of the world.
Mother (me):   That's interesting. But they don't know all about it yet.
Maggie: No. It's mostly hypotheses.
Mother: What do you mean by that?
Maggie: It's what a scientist *thinks might* be true. (Pause.) But we like to believe them, so we won't be too full of wonders.

Being "too full of wonders" is one of the likeliest hazards for a healthy child; whereas the atrophy of wonder is the greatest danger of adulthood.

---

*I believe that most play is embraced by this definition, even "manipulative" play, if the blocks, rocks, etc. are imbued—perhaps silently, internally—with character; even such games as baseball, if the children fancy themselves out of their street or corner lot into some more dazzling diamond where mythic pennants are sought.

"It is axiomatic," writes Gordon in *Synectics,* "that the child's vision is dulled as he is schooled to the regimented responses which will be expected and required of him in an adult world." Some children reveal an early—even resigned—awareness of their impending loss of power. I heard a 4-year-old (defending her purple sky to a chatty woman in a beauty salon) say, "I'll color the way I want now, because when I get to school I'll have to color it the way they say." Calmly. And a 6-year-old once confided, "My curiosity sure can get me into some bad trouble. I wish Santa would sprinkle some magic dust over me so I wouldn't be so curious." (The irony of Santa and wishes being invoked by a child to rob her of her own childhood is a terrible twist.) How much insight can that "child's vision" give us if we see it with a renewed wonder of our own? Children have much to learn—and initially a strong desire to learn it all—from adults; it is also true that adults have much to learn from children, from the very moment of recognizing that fact.

"I am four people in one," said a 7-year-old, "a chemist, an inventor, a scientist, and an astronomer—mostly an astronomer." "I enjoy writing stories," explains a 6-year-old, "but I can't write the words fast enough." Gregg, 5: "I made a terrarium for my frog. It came from my head. . . . No, I didn't have a book to look at. It came from my head." And, flamboyantly crayoning a large paper: "Look't! I'm writing a picture today!" The child in play, says Ruth Hartley, is "externalizing his inner drama—the various aspects of his inner personality—in just the way in which the creative artist in literature or painting does."

Children—in the rather wistful words of a college sophomore— "are busy making a life for themselves; they can be and do anything they want, and nobody thinks they are crazy; they are just children, going wherever their minds take them." His deceptively simple, concise statement contains much of the definition of the child's play. "They are busy": the constant, dedicated absorption; "making": the creating, originating, inventing; "a life for themselves": the vital privacy, purity, unconsciousness of outside demands or extrinsic goals; "they can be and do anything they want": the total freedom to experiment, to become and to enact the full range of possibilities; "and nobody thinks they are crazy": immunity from judgment, poetic license, the deep sanity of allowing free mental range, unconfined, unpatterned; "going wherever their minds take them": liberty, pursuit of happiness. Doing, making, going: play is *active,* as contrasted with passive.

Two small boys sat behind us at the ballgame last Saturday and during the second half of the game the smallest fell asleep and slept through all the cheering and general noise. The other child, who appeared to be about 7 years of age, became restless and wanted to leave. His mother told him to sit still and watch the game. She said, "You like to play football, so why don't you like to watch it?" He answered, "It's more fun to play than to watch."

Lisa, 5 years old, was sitting in a small rocking chair next to her father. Everyone in the living room was watching "The Land of The Giants" on television. Lisa was jumping around in her chair, doing a quiet humming accompaniment to herself. Her mother said, "Lisa, sit still and be quiet so we can hear this show." Lisa said, "That's O.K." Then she let out a sigh, looked at the television set, and said, "Yep, Shut Up—that's the name of the game."

The need for action; 5-year-olds are not spectators, but players. However much good there may be in television, is there too much watching and too little doing in the lives of American children? "I don't like to sit a long time; I like to move around," a 7-year-old explained.

It is a stimulant—perhaps even a condition—of the active character of true play that it is generated out of what adults usually call "nothing." "If you want to see what children can do, you must stop giving them things," says Norman Douglas in a fascinating book called *London Street Games,* "because of course they only invent games when they have none ready-made for them, like richer folks have." Bertrand Russell writes: "The pleasures of childhood should in the main be such as the child extracts himself from his environment by means of some effort and inventiveness. We are creatures of Earth. . . ." "That's what keeps them alive and imaginative," Douglas goes on, "—having nothing to play with; that's what makes them use up all they can find."

Play is *imitation of life.* "We do what we know," stated 8-year-old Cynthia. By observing and representing what surrounds him, the child makes himself "at home in new worlds," in Emerson's words. He makes the familiar new, and the strange familiar.

Play is *imagining, transforming.* Cynthia went on to say, "and we continue with our imagination. We aren't old enough to know all the real things to do, so we just make them up." A discussion of playing among 7-year-olds evoked such remarks as these:

I like to do it because I use my own imagination.
I get to act the way I want.

I can be what I want.
It's like going to Dreamland, and going to Dreamland is like going
to be someone else.
You use your own head.
You pick what you want to be.
You can be anything you want.

The power to originate, the freedom of choice, of experimenting with
impunity, of imagining, are intrinsic to true play. In Richard Adams'
Shardik, the hero Kelderek—battered and exhausted from his long suf-
ferings and trials—finds himself once again playing with a group of children on the riverbank:

> . . . he felt once more, as he had not for years, the exhilara-
> tion of that spontaneity, directness, and absorption that had once
> led him to call children "the flames of God."

Children are also capable of very down-to-earth insights into the
purposes of this play. An 8-year-old: "When you're little and you play
something, you might learn to like it. When you grow up, this might be
the way you choose what you want to do." An unforgettable favorite
cartoon of mine pictures two little boys in knee britches sailing paper
airplanes around the kitchen while their schoolbooks lie abandoned on
the round table; Mama, aproned, hands on hips: "Orville and Wilbur,
stop fooling around and get busy on your homework!"

Play can indeed equal work in dignity and value, and it *is* preparation for later life. Some 10-year-old boys even explained to me, "You can
die without really dying. . . . It's something that happens to everybody
sooner or later, so it's good to know something about it ahead of time."
To rehearse not only life, but also death! A long perspective for people
in their first decade. And a 6-year-old said, "I was never not born." Imitation, imagination, transformation.

> "The impossible and the possible mingle. The conscious does
> not differ from the sub-conscious. The universe is not yet ordered
> according to the laws of reason, but the individual is aware of it in
> each of its manifestations. It is the individual himself. Matter is
> alive; everything is real, nothing is real. And this chaos, far from
> astonishing the child . . . seems natural to him, as if he remembered
> passing through it himself some twenty thousand years ago."
>
> Paul Hazard

The Method

Essentially, that introduces us to the *matter,* plain and complicated. The *method* was always—in the beginning of each term, with each new group of students—regarded by some as madness. At first intuitively, later on deliberately, I would issue an invitation (assignment?) to watch children playing: not organized games like baseball so much as their own playing—spontaneous, self-generated, undirected, private. This request was made early, with almost no preparation, no definitions or explanations of dramatic play. The students were asked to record in writing what they saw and heard of this playing—not clinically, but as truly as possible and in their own ways. My purpose was to force the students into their own genuine, fresh encounters with the phenomena of childhood and natural play. Many were initially puzzled, some craved a questionnaire or outline; but I early sensed and later knew that to submit to telling them "what to look for" and "how to write it" would rob them in advance of their chances of discovery and insight. It was essential for them to look again and listen again to childhood with their *own* eyes, ears, minds; the programming which they so yearned for (out of habit) would have blinded and deafened them to one degree or another. From the most perceptive of them, I always hoped for something approaching 20/20 vision and perfect pitch—if only they could be pressed or wheedled into falling back on their own native faculties—yes, like the children. And many turned out—later or sooner—to be very keen indeed.

As the students' written observations came in, I would select significant and vivid bits (sometimes the whole of a long account), and then read them aloud in class, always preserving anonymity for the freedom and trust of pooling the research—some of which might be quite personal. From the specific, real evidence that emerged, we figured out through free/directed discussion what these happenings seemed to be revealing. Heightened awareness and excitement and floods of memory would sometimes permeate these discussions. But it is needful, after all, to do what I am saying, and let the students speak on their work for themselves—for example:

> . . . Ann (8) looked at me a long time, and then said, "I don't want you to ever get married—stay just like you are forever and ever." Mike (7) said, "All girls get crabby when they get married." These are signs of how children see grownups. It is sad how, as we grow older, we become insensitive to children's feelings. . . . I

vowed to myself when I was about 10 that I would always remember how terrible I felt in certain situations that adults didn't understand. I wanted to be the adult that really understood how kids felt. As the years passed, these feelings dimmed. But now I have realized this before it got too late to remember. I now like to think that I am regaining my sensitivity to children's ideas and feelings. I hope I will stay that way—even after I marry!

Now that I've been watching children play, I've come to believe that every human being—regardless of age, sex, or mental development—has something to offer the world.

I know now that I will be good with children—that sounds terribly conceited and lofty; but I know it. I know it in my very inner soul—that I will get on with them well. These papers have been such an effort—it takes tremendous energy to write them—but it's good, it's *good* energy. And now part of my inner being is immortal on paper.

With children, sensing—yes, sort of like sixth-sensing—and really, really watching are mandatory. . . . The prospect of being a real teacher and having my own class and getting to try things with them makes me feel like I'm full of electricity. And I'm the one who stated flatly that she couldn't do that first assignment, because she never saw children—remember?

I think, watching the children, we're all turned on to life.

Karl (5 years old)—deeply involved in the application of red paint to the paper . . . "This is a big tunnel and I'm inside and I'm lost . . ." (the paint brush was going round and round) "There's a big storm coming." (big splash of red paint) "Here's my mom, she's looking for me. She can't find me; she's got a flashlight . . . " (a small spot of white paper is showing through the red paint) "I'm scared, my mom's hollering and it's getting dark . . . " (more red paint—a sigh) "Oh, boy! She didn't find me."

And some people might have said that painting was of *nothing*.

So now, from the abundance gathered with the vastly varied help of nearly 3,000 students over a period of 14 years, samples have been selected to bring together a representative range of accounts of children playing. The promise and practice of privacy has been carried over from classroom to book; authors of individual segments are not separately identified. And for every entry included, scores of others, by other students have had to be left out. Some segments have been chosen because they represent such characteristic forms of play as to be classic; others because they are unique, and therefore demonstrate the infinite individuality of children. The collection as a whole seeks to embrace most of the essential characteristics of children's dramatic play, through the compelling medium of direct evidence seen by many eyes.

"Life is a flow, not a file," says Fadiman. Amen. This seething life-process that we are contemplating refuses, like the children who do it, to be still and be categorized. Yet in the flow that follows is an order and a design which, it is hoped, will take us a bit closer to understanding play as a microcosm of life itself.

Recapture of, re-entry into the world of child's play is—for those who have lost the way—essential to whatever they may plan and hope to do as grown-ups in the "real" world. For anyone interested in teaching, in theatre/drama, in loving, in parenting—for them it is primary, fundamental. The first step, back into the sources of life.

It is no accident, of course—presumptuous as it may seem—that I have interwoven quotations of Einstein and Aristotle with those of Ypsilanti students and children from the mud-puddles of Michigan. It is no small part of my point that wisdom is where you find it, and that all of us, young and old, small and great, must combine forces in seeking to understand and improve the human condition.

CHAPTER TWO

....

Imitation of Life

"We do what we know . . . "

       Cynthia (8 years old), during a discussion of dramatic play.

"An artist is a dreamer consenting to dream of the actual world."

       Santayana

"Imitation is natural to man from childhood, one of his advantages over the lower animals being this, that he is the most imitative creature in the world, and learns at first by imitation. And it is also natural for all to delight in works of imitation. The truth of this second point is shown by experience: though the objects themselves may be painful to see, we delight . . . in the most realistic representations of them in art. . . The explanation is to be found in a further fact: to be learning something is the greatest of pleasures not only to the philosopher but also to the rest of mankind, however small their capacity for it . . . the reason of the delight . . . is . . . gathering the meaning of things . . . "

       Aristotle, *Poetics*

    Some of our most ancient wisdom, some of the plainest of truths, are at times forgotten or undervalued. Recent decades have echoed and reechoed the word "creative" in all of its forms ("-ivity" perhaps the most prominent). The name for that most god-like act has all but lost its meaning in a flood of routine, fill-in-the-blanks, pre-packaged "activity" prescriptions so *other* than creative as to amount to double-think.

    Ironically, one backlash of the "creativity" craze has been the neglect, the ignoring of *imitation*—with all of its implications—in human learning and art. If "creative" has come to mean panacea in current language, "imitative" has, I suspect, almost come to mean anathema. "Imitation" must be restored to its rightful, essential place in our studies of the human condition; it has been probed from Aristotle to Piaget as a fundamental process whose intricate mysteries we have yet to understand, but have always used.

To imitate, "to hold the mirror up to nature" requires, after all, a complex operation beginning with the child's selective observation of the world around and within himself, melding into the absorption of this data, a recombining and interpreting of it, and a *reproduction* of some new arrangement of it. Imitation can never be total or exact, of course (rarely needs to be), but the high fidelity of some of the detail copied and reenacted in children's play continues to astonish the attentive adult eye and ear. (Inevitably, we have forgotten some of what we intuitively knew ourselves as children: a loss; but also, the perspective of time and maturity discovers values in play that could never occur to a child's mind.)

Freud writes that "the play of children is determined by their wishes—really by the child's one wish, which is to be grown-up, the wish that helps to 'bring him up.' He always plays at being grownup; in play he imitates what is known to him of the lives of adults." "I believe," writes an E.M.U. sophomore (innocent of, unaided by Freud), "that children do everything they do in play because of a desire to be an adult. It seems that their play is full of meaning, and represents all kinds of problems which they will face when they are grown up." From two different centuries, two different continents, these two crystal-clear statements express the same fundamental fact: a fact whose significance is far greater than is commonly understood.

The following observations by students may throw light on this natural tendency of children in play to *imitate* and *re-present* what they see and hear of the adult world.

> Whenever I go home I have a chance to see my brothers and sisters at play. Their play often consists of imitating adult actions. My younger sister still plays dolls. She is 9 years old. When playing with her doll she *copies* in great detail the actions of a mother caring for her child. She changes the diapers, feeds her doll, talks to it. This doll isn't one that cries and talks and winks; this doll is an old-fashioned doll that does what the child's mind can do. My sister also likes to dress in my mother's things: her old high heels, rings, necklaces, hats, dresses. . . . She doesn't just stick to things that mothers do in the house. She likes to take part in things which are usually labelled as things that boys do; she likes to be on a pirate ship or help build a tree fort or club-house. She hasn't reached the age yet where she must just be a girl. She can do whatever she wants and go wherever her mind takes her.

One afternoon . . . while walking back towards campus I saw a little girl, a little boy, and a turned-over shopping cart. The girl was shaking her finger in the boy's face; in her other hand was a muddy doll: "You should never leave a baby alone!" she said. The boy looked very crestfallen when she went on, "See if I ever marry you again."

I came in from school one day and found Becky (2 years old) sitting on my bed with one of my books open in her lap. The first thing she said to me was, "Don't make noise; I reading book." I realized that that is what I usually say to her when she comes into my room.

My little sister Darla, age 9, was playing the customary "House" with her first-grade friend Meg. Darla said: "O.K. Meg, you be George and I'll be Lottie."
George and Lottie are the names of my parents. That same day later on, I heard Meg say, "Let's play George and Lottie." Now I've seen Darla play "House and Family" a thousand times, and I don't know why I didn't notice it before: that she always used the same names for the husband and wife, and also for the children. All of Darla's dolls were named after my brothers and sisters. . . . Meg even let her stomach hang loose so that she'd have the "pot-belly" like my dad.

Thursday, three little girls (about 8 years old, I think) were playing house on a big front porch. They were all dressed up in grown-up clothes, including heels, hats, and purses. About ten feet away there was a little boy playing all by himself. He looked very bored. All of a sudden he ran up on the porch where the girls were playing. One little girl greeted him with the following remark: "John, get out of here. You are the father and you are not supposed to be home from work yet."

Location: Kindergarten room, Lincoln Park. There is a "doll corner" in the room, with a stove, a sink, a table, and chairs. There are dishes on the table. Four boys and one girl are in this corner. The girl is wearing high heels and is pushing a doll carriage. She raises a finger to her mouth, stamps her foot, and tells the boys to s-s-s-s-h. Now she is bending over the buggy and is talking to the two dolls; now tucks the blanket around them. The first boy is wearing a man's old felt hat and has a man's necktie draped over his shoulders. He tries but cannot manage to knot the tie so he just loops it. He is standing at the kitchen sink, has a glass in one hand and an empty bottle in the other; says he is "mixing a drink."
The second boy is "cooking" at the stove. He is talking to the boy at the sink, too quietly for me to catch the words. There is a great deal of body motion while he stirs imaginary ingredients in a pan.

The third boy is sitting in a rocking chair and leans over to look at the dolls in the buggy. Now he is staring straight ahead and quietly rocks in his chair.

The fourth boy is using the play phone. His legs are crossed and one elbow rests on his knee while he quietly, seriously carries on his conversation. With one hand he wipes his brow and then scratches his head. He does not pay any attention to the other children in the corner.

Three of the boys go out of the house and walk around the classroom with their "motors" running—a sound coming out of the mouth. The girl also leaves the house, pushing the buggy all around the room.

Two other girls now enter this corner. They have put ladies' hats on and are sitting down to the table. Politely they pass the sugar bowl, the silverware, and the cookie tray; I hear "please" and "thank you." Vigorous stirring of the spoon in the cup! Little fingers are held in rigid upright position while drinking from the cup. They smack their lips and smile at each other. One girl passes empty plate, saying, "Honey, here's another cookie."

A new boy enters—raises his hands in the air, then drops them to his sides and says, "What a day! What a day!" Now he picks up a small broom and begins to sweep the floor.

Meanwhile, the boy in the rocking chair, apparently deep in thought, continues to rock.

The dialog below took place during free time in the playhouse. Barbara (9 years old) was the mother, and had on huge red clip-on earrings and junk beads. Bradley (8) used one of the boys' hats, and kept it on constantly—he was the father. Donny (6) and Rhonda (6) wore only their own clothes—they were the children.

Barb:	Let's play house, Rhonda.
Brad:	I'm the father (putting on the hat). Donny, you be my boy.
Don:	I'm always the baby. Why can't I be father?
Brad:	I'm bigger than you. Besides, Barbara is taller than you.
Don:	I'm always a little kid. I don't want to be a little kid again.
Barb:	I know. You can be the older brother and go to work with Bradley. Here, Rhonda, you be my little girl. (Rhonda just quietly followed Barbara around.)
Brad:	O.K., Honey, time to go to work. Haven't you got my lunchbox ready yet?
Barb:	No, stupid. You haven't eaten breakfast yet. Common' Rhonda, help me set this table.
Rhonda:	O.K. (Rhonda sets table as Barbara is at the stove —pretending to make breakfast and getting lunches ready.)
Don:	What am I gonna get for lunch?
Barb:	You're supposed to call me "Mother."

Don:	O.K., Mom, what am I gonna eat for lunch today? I don't want no peanut-butter today.
Barb:	I'm giving you ham sandwiches today, Donny. Is that all right?
Don:	Oh, good! I'm sick of peanut-butter.
	(Bradley is at the table. Rhonda is just sitting down.)
Brad:	Hurry up the breakfast. Sit down, Donny. We're gonna be late.
Barb:	Oh, here it is. Scrambled eggs, bacon, milk for Donny and Rhonda and coffee for us.
Don:	I thought I wasn't gonna be a little kid. Why do I get milk?
Brad:	If you want coffee, hurry up and get it or we'll be late.
	(Donny decides to drink the milk.)
	(Everyone is eating.)
Brad:	Rhonda, you be good in school today. No more talking like you did yesterday.
Rhonda:	O.K., but I'm always a good girl.
Barb:	O.K. Breakfast is over. You three go now or you'll be late.
	(Everyone gets up. Barbara hands them their make-believe lunches and tells them they can go.)
Don:	Aren't you going to kiss Mom, Father?
Brad:	We're only playing, Donny.

I have an 18-month-old niece who is just beginning to use sentences (about five words at most). She copies every move and sound her father makes. (For example, her father stands with his feet shoulder-width apart and his hands clasped behind his back; this is how Wendy stands.) She doesn't function as just an instant replay; she does her feed-back hours, even days later.

During the football season, Bob (W's father) spent a lot of time "glued" to the T.V. games. He would become very involved with the plays, and at exceptionally well-executed ones he would shout "God! Was that a great play!" One Sunday morning in church there was a baptism, the first that Wendy had ever seen. As the minister was sprinkling the water over the baby's head, Wendy's voice was clearly heard all over the church: "God! Was that a great play!"

The other evening when we were visiting their house, Wendy was walking around the house with her fist against her ear, saying, "Yeah! Yeah? Yeah. No! Yeah?" (During this time her head was nodding up and down.) When she finished we asked her who she was talking to. She replied, "To my booze." Of course, she meant "boss"—we think—but "booze" is a frequent word of her father's. As everyone started to laugh, she looked confused, then hurt. She was trying her hardest to act grown up, and we were laughing at her. No wonder children get discouraged growing up.

I remember very clearly a boy who was in my kindergarten class. During "Free Play" the boys would usually play with the trucks, blocks, or tricycles. The girls would play house, store, school, or nurse. However, Dave would always be with the girls who were playing house. He would sit on a chair and slide (push) himself all over the "house." We girls always thought he was odd because he was always underfoot whenever we tried to do anything in our "house." We ended up just ignoring him.

As I grew older I forgot about Dave's play habits until once during my high school days I went to a party at his home and met his parents. His father was confined to a wheel chair and had been for over 12 years. I then remembered Dave's "playing" and realized that he was playing the adult male role the best and only way he at that time knew how.

I am in Campus Service Corps and a group leader of six small children (6-year-olds) from Perry School. It is with these six children that I have seen the most dramatic play. Recently I had the opportunity to be what the kids called "special visitor" to their operating room. The room consisted of a huge cardboard box that would hold four small children comfortably. The "special visitor" watched what went on in the operating room through a crudely cut-out window on the side of the box. Stacy was lying on the floor part of the box and on her stomach was a balloon with a blanket draped over her body. This gave the effect that Stacy was "expectin' a baby." Denise and Annie were the nurses, while Joe was the doctor. Stacy then began to whimper and toss on the floor and the "Doctor" exclaimed, "Hurry up-nurse-the-baby's-acomin'!" No sooner had this been said than Annie produced a wet doll which she hurriedly wrapped in a blanket. "It's a boy," Joe screamed, "but he won't have a ma, she's lookin' awful." Then the next thing I knew Denise was putting the blanket over Stacy's head. I was truly amazed and a little frightened over what I had just witnessed. I later learned that Stacy's 15-year-old unmarried sister had died during childbirth while Stacy was in the next bed. It was hard for me to believe that a child only 6 years old had seen someone close to her die.

A group of 6 and 7-year-old boys were playing with toy guns and when I stopped and asked them what they were playing, they said they were "getting prepared in case of a *serious* attack."

Rackham School (Special Education)

I slipped into a classroom to observe 4- and 5-year-olds, explaining to the student teacher there that I was hoping to see their dramatic play. She said pleasantly, "Good luck. These children have language problems." I subsequently found that their scant speech was not as much a handicap to them as it was to me, since I lacked those verbal clues that help an adult to interpret what "they are about." But there was plenty of play; for example:

Two girls seat themselves side by side at a round table, with dolls lying on the table in front of them. Girl 1 offers her baby a small plastic turtle in a "have a drink" motion. Girl 2 hands Girl 1 a small building block, takes one herself, and both offer them to the dolls as if feeding them. They exchange smiles. Girl 2 says, "Babys' crying," and picks up the doll, lays it over her shoulder, and pats it gently. Girl 1 does likewise.

Sharon, who loves to play with dolls, said, "I've got enough education because I've been going to school for two years. I just want to be a Mama anyhow."

Two little girls about 7 years old were walking their babies. They were dressed in long dresses, a curtain was draped over one girl's shoulder, wide brimmed hats sat on each blond head, their ankles turned often in their high heeled shoes, and they each carried a handbag. They pushed the carriages and looked in several times and made adjustments. The taller girl spoke to her baby as she bent over the carriage. As she straightened up she said, "You know Bobbie is getting a tooth and he is so fussy." They continued walking to the end of the block and then they turned around. As they passed again the smaller "mother" was asking her friend to come over for coffee. "Well, just for a minute—I have to start dinner; we bowl tonight."

I have less difficulty in observing dramatic play than in under-standing the quality and depth of what I see and hear. While shop-ping this evening I noticed two girls (probably between 4 and 5 years old) talking. One had her mother's purse. The smaller girl was posing toward a three-way mirror, regarding herself at various angles. Both girls tried to stand on their toes as much as possible (perhaps to simulate high heels). This is what I heard:

Isn't this a beautiful dress?
I don't think it's you.
But I like the midi length.
I think you should get a mini-skirt dress. That would be sexy.
But Richard doesn't like me in short skirts.
How much does it cost?
It costs a thousand hundred dollars.
That's too much.
I won't get it because Richard doesn't like me to charge too
    much all the time.
Let's go eat lunch. I'm getting a Whopper.
I'm on a diet so don't let me order calories.

On the playground a few first grade girls were reenacting their gym class, which I had just observed. In class they had learned some ballet steps. One girl acted as teacher while the rest lined up opposite her. She would call out various steps and walk around hitting each girl on the knees and feet, yelling at them as she went. When one complained, she said, "That's how Teacher does it."

During a session of "playing school" in our back yard, one of the "pupils" (5-year-old Debbie) questioned the "teacher" (my 8-year-old son Troy) as to why she had to do what he'd just ordered her to do. My son the "teacher" replied: "I'm not going to tell you *why*! There are some rules children aren't supposed to understand!"

Matthew (5 years old) told me he was going to teach Kathy and Rhonda how to climb. I said, "They're not supposed to climb." "I know it," he said disgustedly, "but I'm going to teach them for when they're big as me."

Joseph has always been the quiet and sometimes hostile one in the group. Before Halloween the kids were making costumes out of paper bags, paper plates, straws and other things. Joe began to work on a costume that consisted of a bullet proof vest, a knife, and a gun. He became a robber and began to steal little things from the other children. As he returned them he screamed "Here come the cops, here come the cops and I ain't done nothin'. wrong." Then he would clutch his head and fall to the ground. Joe's brother was killed in a street gang raid in New York City.

As I was walking from class, up by Roosevelt, two boys, about fourth or fifth graders, approached me. They both had sticks in their hands, which they told me were microphones. They told me that I looked like a young lady who was concerned about what was going on in the world and that they would like to ask me a few questions. They explained that their names were Huntley and Brinkley and asked me what I thought of the war in Viet Nam. After I answered this question for them, they went on to ask me if I thought that school was necessary, and shouldn't there be more and longer vacations, and more recesses and shorter school days. I said this sounded very much like a labor union making demands to the labor management. They thanked me for my opinions and then moved on to question others.

The car was bigger than Robert (5 years old), but he managed to push it over near the sink. He couldn't ride and steer because his feet wouldn't reach the ground to provide the power. Keeping one eye on his property, he hauled several large blocks to his car. The first blocks were stacked laboriously, and one of the car ends was hoisted into position. This was repeated for the back end. Robert got a bowl from the play house, filled it with water, and dropping in a sponge, carried it to the car. He had done all this without one word or offer of aid from the teachers or other children. After he had been scrubbing his car for ten minutes, I asked if he was planning a trip. Robert replied that he was a "car wash," and continued to slop with abandon. He dismissed me, saying, "Can't talk now." Ricky, Darryl, and David eventually came to help, but Robert screamed and they retreated. The boys returned with their own cars, water, and sponges. Newspaper was put down to stop the river from spreading, and the boys played Car Wash for more than an hour.

The following day we took a trip to a real Car Wash, and watched the teacher's car go through. They were impressed by the fact that the men dried the car after it had been washed. In all subsequent Car Washes (and there were many) the cars were dried with paper towels. I think one reason Car Wash is still so popular is that it allows water play in a masculine setting, and is something that can be done by all the children.

Krogers—two girls (about 10 years old)
"Hi, I'm Betty Furness, and I'm here to tell you about new Thrill for dishes," said one, holding up a container. (The other girl stopped her cart to listen.) "It makes your hands smooth and nice and soft—and it's good for your dishes." The second girl laughed with evident delight, then said seriously: "I've been using Brand X for years, and I love it."

"Well, maybe you have, but if you want your dishes really clean, then you will buy this new Thrill."

As the two girls walked past me with their cart, the last thing I heard was, "Let's go over to the cookie counter—I know a good one for Oreos."

Two little neighbor girls, age 4, rang our doorbell and when my mother answered the door, they told her that they were selling "pretty rocks" and asked if she would like to buy some. She said no, she didn't think so today, and then they told her that they were only "two pennies for a whole handful." So my mother said, "Well, what can I do with these pretty rocks?" The children then told her that she could use them for anything she wanted—she could put them in the fish's bowl (we do not have a fish, but both of them do), since "all fish like to have pretty rocks in their bowls," she could "put them on top of the dirt in a flower plot," because one child's

mother does this, or she could "put them in a jar and set them on the table for people to look at because they are pretty." My mother then bought four handfuls of the pretty rocks; the children watched her place them in a jar and set them on the table. After they had gone, she told me that a door-to-door salesman had just come around the neighborhood.

The three boys ranged from 6 to 8 years of age. When I chanced along, they were deeply engaged in a game of war. The foe was imaginary. What struck me most was the emphasis they seemed to place on death: being hit by a bullet was acted out through body, face, voice.

I don't know how many times I have watched little boys (not girls!) playing this same game, but I began to realize now how much more there is to their playing than meets the eye. These children are a reflection of our society; they are living proof of what we have created. Already they know about machine guns and grenades.

My grand-daughter, Bethany, playing Store with another 4-year-old: "You know, a penny won't buy much now." "I'll take some candy—it's good to keep the children quiet."

From House through School to Store; from childbirth to death, this *imitation of life* through children's dramatic play moves on as naturally as the tides. It goes on in the streets and alleys of Rome, Paris, and London (I have watched it there) as well as in the back yards, the basements, and the sidewalks of America. It is the child's way of studying life itself; studying this play can be the discerning adult's way of learning more about both the "reality" reflected and the "seer" reflecting—the child in the act of trying to "hold the mirror up to nature."

The amazing *detail* which proliferates in dramatic play as the child develops is in itself worth noticing at this point. Extreme, patient attention is sometimes paid to the paraphernalia (the "props") and the regulations involved in the imitation. Hours, days, even weeks can be spent on elaborating these structures, physical and/or organizational. "Library" can involve carefully kept check-out cards; playhouses or club headquarters can evolve intricate equipment and systems of rules.

Today we went to visit friends. They have a 10-year-old girl and an 11-year-old boy. They showed my girls their newest treasure—homemade spy kits. They are all the rage now. I watched as they explained the contents. The girl's was a cosmetic case containing:

1. Purse filled with fake jewelry to replace the real thing.
2. Pad of paper for notes and codes.
3. Box with a clicker in it for sending Morse code.
4. Book of Codes and Secret Writing.
5. Pea shooter.
6. Super-Stuff for taking finger prints.
7. Code club card.
8. I.D. card with picture.
9. Walkie talkie—also used as a disguised gun.
10. Sun glasses.
11. Candle.
12. Play money to bribe.
13. Tweezers for picking up bombs.
14. Compass for finding bombs.
15. Rocket from G.I. Joe set for tear gas.
16. Molder—this is a plastic rainhat case. You put 2 ends of a broken chain or wire in it and it molds them together.

The boy's kit is in a camera box and contains:

1. Small chess set as a computer.
2. Night-light is an ultra violet light.
3. Gun.
4. Tube of glue for bomb.
5. Bomb from G.I. Joe set.
6. Money.
7. Extra bullets.
8. Clip is a mike that can be attached to the enemy when you walk past him so you can monitor what he says.
9. Harmonica—you can play it when you are in jail.
10. Film box holds small roll of paper for sending secret messages.

I can always remember playing teacher, but my sister Darla (7) surprised me one day by asking me if I wanted to play secretary. Darla had made a typewriter out of an empty shoe box. A roll from paper toweling became the carriage return and a piece of ribbon became the typing ribbon. Inside of the box there were quite a few sheets of paper that she had printed up before which acted as her typed-out papers. She just pulled one out after she had "typed" out a letter or something. It was quite elaborate. She also had made a telephone out of paper cups and a pencil sharpener out of an old fruit juice can. There were about ten already sharpened pencils in the can so that when Darla went to sharpen one of her pencils all that she had to do was pull out one that was in the can.

My 10-year-old, Nancy, came home with a list of requirements for belonging to the witch club. . . . She made up a witch test and gave it out to the other members:

1. Know how to zapp people.
2. Know how to climb high places.
3. Eat certain foods like: fruit, vegetables, toast with jam, corn flakes once a week, meat.
4. If you're a witch then act like one.
5. You cannot zapp people unless you have a pen mark on your finger.
6. If you're a witch then don't talk to anyone else.
7. If you're a witch then you have to steal once a week—something not very important. (I asked her about this one and she said that it would only be a piece of paper or something like that.)
8. Bring in the thing stolen and pay 2¢ dues.
9. Come every Saturday to Bonnie's house.
10. Take a bath once a week and comb your hair every day. (I told her she takes a bath more than once a week and she

said that's because I make her; this once a week is the way
they want it.)
11. Know how to fly through the air.

Literature as a form of life experience is also "imitated" in children's
dramatic play. Whole books, of course, have been devoted to this aspect of the subject, but it nevertheless must be included here as well. Its
importance is too vast to measure, since it expands the realm of the
child's vision past what he has "actually" observed, to reach or at least
glimpse places, times, people he cannot directly know. Indeed in fantasy, myth, science fiction, the worlds that he can reflect and study may
be beyond what *anyone* has literally known. The child can thus satisfy
such "primordial human desires" as "to survey the depths of time and
space," and "to hold communion with other living things." (Tolkien)

Not surprisingly, elements of the literature encountered are spontaneously selected and arranged by children in infinitely varied individual ways. Here are just a few representative examples of dramatic
play imitating literature:

> I had stopped in at my cousin's house to deliver a package.
> As I walked in the back door I saw my little 4-year-old cousin Karen
> dressed at the bottom of the basement stairs with a green and yel-
> low jersey flowered skirt and blouse on. My cousin came upstairs
> and we sat at the kitchen table to talk. Within a few minutes Karen
> and Colleen, who is 3, danced around the room behind us. Karen
> was Cinderella dancing at the ball and Colleen was the prince. Col-
> leen was dressed in play clothes. Suddenly a gong was heard com-
> ing from Karen's mouth and she announced, "It's midnight, it's
> midnight, I have to hurry home or I'll turn into a witch." She ran
> into the front room, leaving one high heeled shoe behind for the
> prince to find. Then she came back and told the prince he had "to
> find the person that fit the shoe." Colleen came over to me and told
> me to take off my shoes because she had to find out if it fit. No, it
> didn't fit. She went to her mother. No, it didn't fit again. Then she
> went to her sister Kathy, who is 8. No, it didn't fit her either. "Try it
> on my foot" said Karen. Colleen did and the shoe fit. There was a
> moment of joyous laughter then the prince and Cinderella went
> skipping off into the front room together.

> I work at the Southfield Public Library. . . . One day two boys,
> about 9 and 10 came in. . . . When I noticed that they were still wan-
> dering around "lost" I went over to ask if I could help them. One
> boy (I learned later that his name was Bob) ventured, "We'd like
> some books, but there's so many!" The other—Tim—happened to

glance up to see a display on mythology, and seemed interested in it. Thanks to my four years of Latin, I was able to tell them about the Trojan War, and then I gave them each a copy of a child's version of the *Iliad*. They wanted explanations of many of the illustrations. Finally, the boys were satisfied with their selections, and I checked all of their books out for them.

Next to the library is a small play area for children. 1 could hear a lot of yelling from that direction, and when I looked out the window, there were Bob and Tim, reenacting the battle of Achilles and Hector from the *Iliad*. Tim was standing (on the jungle gym) above Bob as Hector had stood on the walls of Troy when Achilles challenged him. Then the battle began, with each of the boys calling on his "divine protector." I watched at the window, amazed, as they repeated every last detail that I had told them. Just at the victory of Achilles, the honking of a car horn brought them back to the present, and, gathering up their books, off they went. I stood there wondering what other great adventures they could have with those books that they had taken out of a Southfield, Michigan library

For several weeks my 11-year-old has been reading books about witches—for example: *The Little Left-Over Witch*.

These have inspired her to live in the closet, color only with black crayon, dress in as much black as possible; in general, think witch. She regularly takes her blanket, pillow, radio, lamp, treats, and books into the closet and closes the door.

I stopped at a friend's house and while I was there her sixth grade sister and three friends were playing princess. One girl was the mean princess and the others were her loyal servants. She commanded, "Maid, maid I want my tea now." "Yes, my princess," they answered and brought her a cup. "That's much too hot," she said when she tasted it. "Bring me another, and this time not so hot." They got her another. "This one is too cold! You worthless servants are trying to kill me. Don't you know any better?" She jumped up and began beating them with her rope "whip." She "killed" the unworthy servants and they all went to get something to eat.

We'd been reading one of their favorite Lois Lenski books, *Cowboy Small;* the group had been worried about the cow being branded. It was explained that this mark showed that the cow belonged to Cowboy Small, and if the cow was ever lost, the people who found it could know it was Cowboy Small's and return it. We showed that Cowboy Small's horse had the same brand.

Several days later David and Leslie (4) . . . built horses of large blocks, and David was saddling his with the rest mats. I patted his horse, said it was a good looking horse, and asked if I could buy it. "No," said David in a gruff voice, "I hafta see my cows." He jumped on his horse, reached behind him, and fastened something in front of him. "Your guns?" "No, seat belts." "Pretty modern horse, Cowboy." "There's a transistor in the back for music." And turning on his radio, extending his left arm to signal a turn, Cowboy David galloped off after his cows. Leslie fastened his seat belt and charged after David. When Leslie's bouncing dislodged the saddle and he fell off the horse, they decided to continue their search on foot.

"Guire, will you be my cow?" Leslie asked. I started to MOO-oo-oo and Leslie roped me and sat me on the floor. "Now I'll brand you." He dug his fingers into my arm. David admired my brand, but Leslie wouldn't allow him to brand my other arm. Leslie told me, "Now you're my cow; when you're lost they'll bring you home."

This marvelous capacity to *notice,* to *pay attention to* the new evidence that his world continually presents to him, is proven in the child's play over and over again as he works through this "rehearsal of things known," as Winifred Ward has so aptly called it. Dramatic play compellingly demonstrates the child's need and ability to imitate what he observes and remembers of the myriad stimuli swirling around him. Through his play he tries constantly to record and to sort out all that he can of this kaleidoscopic flow.

And, inseparably, he simultaneously reaches for those things he *cannot imitate* because they are not yet known to him—or perhaps to anyone—and for this miraculous act, the child needs a still more potent faculty: *imagination.*

....

CHAPTER THREE

Imagination and Transformation

"We do what we know, and we continue with our imagination."

Cynthia (8-year-old)

" . . . his rehearsal of things known and his exploration of things unknown."

Ward

"Imagination is more powerful than knowledge."

Einstein

"Lovers and madmen have such seething brains,
Such shaping fantasies, that apprehend
More than cool reason ever comprehends."

Shakespeare

"Dream child moving through a world
Of wonders wild and new . . . "

Lewis Carroll

"Know you what it is to be a child? . . . It is to have a spirit still streaming from the waters of baptism . . . it is to turn pumpkins into coaches and mice into horses, lowness into loftiness, and nothing into everything, for each child has its fairy godmother in its soul."

Shelley

"If you have built castles in the air, your work need not be lost; that is where they should be. Now put the foundations under them."

Thoreau

"Momma, I want to go out to play with Prince Charming."

Stacey (7-year-old)

"And as imagination bodies forth
The forms of things unknown, the poet's pen
Turns them to shapes, and gives to airy nothing
A local habitation and a name."

Shakespeare

"Man is the only being that is able to transcend himself."

Dr. Victor Frankl

Transformation! A group of about ten 8-year-olds that I was playing with, effectively and matter-of-factly turned a plain old wooden platform into a raft (on an ocean seething with people-eating crocodiles), a submarine (nearly out of gas and without quite enough oxygen to reach the surface), a time-tunnel, a cage, a floating house in a flood, a boat with a leak, a space ship, a stage with ballet dancers and singers, a magic carpet over eastern places, a balloon (with an air leak), an island with cannibals.

9-year-olds turned a paper towel tube into:
> a telescope
> a hot dog
> Pinnochio's nose when he lied
> a rolling pin
> a worm with rigor mortis
> a horn
> a candle
> French bread
> a bazooka
> a wheel on Flintstone's car
> a baton
> a giant's straw
> a giant's cigarette
> the Leaning Tower of Pisa
> the fat wand of a fat fairy
> a diploma
> the world's biggest piece of bubble gum
> antenna for hearing otherwise unheard things

and much else besides—but lists (even of fascinating things) become tedious if they get too long.

However, one more list is, I think, needed here; a list of a kindred yet somewhat different sort: a list of some (only some!) of the actual objects contained in a children's (7-year-olds) "treasure chest":

empty perfume bottle
football cleat
2-inch clothes brush
works from a watch
keyring
piece of sandstone
empty lipstick container
bicycle handlebar
pine cone
bit of yellow yarn
jacks
scrap of blue cellophane
cereal tokens
boomerang
jar lid
marble (clear)
shoe horn
thimble
sinker
model car hub-cap
rusted barrette
an ignition key
a plastic tape spool
a broken belt buckle
a fossil
a rabbit's foot (fake)
a coil from an electromagnet
nails
an English walnut
connected paper clips
an amber (plastic) comb with most teeth missing
a scarlet ribbon

This authentic (though partial) catalogue is of real objects that in themselves interested these children, but beyond that, these objects contained a *transformational potential* magnetic and compelling to them, as the peanut and the soybean were to George Washington Carver. Most of these child-treasures are a grown-up's trash. "Children are rich with all that they do not own," says Paul Hazard—and the worldly possessions that a child does own ought properly to be (if they are as lucky as Tom and Huckleberry and the owners of the above treasure chest) just such "transformational trash" as is listed above. And earth, air, water: the very Elements themselves.

"*Make-believe*" is a word which, worn out as it may be in some minds, is worth keeping and freshening, because—when considered simply, cleared of any accumulated cuteness—it is potent with meaning. "Make" is a strong, plain word, combining all of the denotations and connotations of both "create" and "compel, require, force." "Believe": the willing, concentrated, self-generated entry into the invented, imagined, inner world where the playing absorbs the mind in its endless experiment. The more these powers are exercised, the more highly they are developed. "Why, I've believed as many as six impossible things before breakfast," the White Queen tells Alice in *Through The Looking Glass,* "I daresay you haven't had much practice; try again!"

And certainly it makes sense (as nonsense reflected so often does) that imagining (what if humans *could* take pictures of Mars?), believing the impossible (this "still" desk *is* in motion), transforming (soybeans *can* turn into tile floors; a human embryo does turn into a full-grown man or woman)—all must be practiced in the ceaseless natural struggle toward mastery.

Now, looking back for a moment, it is clear that all of the instances of dramatic play which were given primarily to demonstrate the process of imitation also embodied imagination. Obviously, the 7-year-old imitating a mother can only do so by transforming herself; by believing that an inanimate doll is a living child, and so on. All of the examples that now follow are chosen to focus on the *imaginative part*—dominant, elaborated—of the playing process; imitation is, of course, still a vital element. Predoomed efforts at neat classification should not be allowed to come between us and our contemplation of this living and therefore restlessly complex phenomenon that we seek to understand a little better.

Sometimes the art of dramatic play makes things out of "thin air" ("airy nothing" into a golden trumpet):

Not long afterwards. . . I happened to hear Willie (6) saying he could play the trumpet. The other boys, Joe and Ben, kept saying they did not believe him. Willie stood up in his place and pretended he had a trumpet in his hands. With sound effects and body movements Willie went through a trumpet rendition that left the boys and me speechless. Willie has never held a real trumpet in his hands. His mother told me that Willie's idol is Louis Armstrong.

Sometimes a physical object is used in the transforming; a swing set becomes a jail:

It was a cold day but the children had gone outside anyway. . . We started running, tagging, and catching games to keep warm.

After catching me Leslie (4) announced, "You go to jail." He took me to the jail (the three supports of the swing set). Leslie slammed the door, saying, "BANG," and locked me in. Then he stated the only rule—"You gotta escape." So I rattled the "door" and shot the "lock" off with my "gun." I was recaptured with the help of Robert, who hung on my leg and was begging to be dragged along the ground. The next escape was while Leslie was sleeping; I knew he was sleeping because while leaning on a jail support with one eye open, he said, "I'm sleeping." I escaped and was recaptured again; then Leslie began using "handcuffs" to haul me to jail. After what proved to be my final capture Leslie, hanging on one arm with Robert clutching both my knees, said I shouldn't be bad and had to go back to jail. Then he said, "Will you come peace'blee?" "Yes." "Well then we won't hold you." He let go and started away, but I couldn't move with Robert still strangling my legs. Leslie charged back, "Boy, let go. Guire said she'd come peace'blee!" So I was escorted to jail. Locking the door Leslie said, "If you are good your family can see you." Lunch time ended my jail sentence. I told one of the teachers that I'd been playing Jail. She explained that Leslie's father was in jail, and would probably be gone for a while. Leslie was 3 when his father was taken from home at night by three policemen. The family, the mother and five children, visit every time they are allowed to. This was the only time we played Jail. This was the only time I have ever seen any child at the Perry preschool be the policeman. Fireman yes, police no.

The jungle gym can be many things to many boys and girls, especially those with running imaginations. One day all the boys were playing on it and suddenly they came running to me yelling "Help! The GIANT SPIDER is after me and he will eat me up." The so called "Giant Spider" was the smallest boy in the class but for a few minutes he was by far the largest.

A 4-year-old put sand on a free-form white sculpture and said, "It's snowing!" Another got on one of the spring-bouncing animals (not a horse) and yelled, "Ride 'em, Cowboy!" He put his index finger out and kept shouting "Pow!"

The second group were 6 and 7 year olds who, their teacher explained, have learning problems. They are capable, but somehow not making progress in school situations.

Several were clustered at the bird-cage climbing bars. . . . Diverse sound effects and announcements of, "I'm Batman, I'm Superman." "Brumm Brumm . . . brumm . . . wow !" They clambered down and went in all directions.

Several boys on some merry-go-round equipment. Boy: "Let's pretend our engine is burning up." They drag their feet in the dust and clouds of "smoke" rise up.

One boy, in a running leap, got astride a large concrete freeform. Another boy following him sang out, "It's a rocket ship." They left and two girls took their places. Girl 1: "This is a horse, you guys!" To the other girls, "I'm riding it, you have to hang on—no seat belt. Pretend you sleep in the day and I sleep in the night." . . . She hums a snatch of the "Lone Ranger" tune and ends her play sliding off with a "Wheeeee."

The wedding was about to begin with the bride waiting at the altar as her husband-to-be was escorted or rather dragged down the aisle by three friends. The 7-year-old couple were united in matrimony with all the solemnity of any make believe wedding.

Instantly came four children: Tom, Rinny, Mike and Larry. Susie was appointed nurse maid and her first duty was to awaken the sleeping boys from their swing type beds and send them out to play, from which they never returned. When Karen, the mother, was asked if she was concerned about them she replied, "They're big boys. They can take care of themselves!"

Other 7-year-olds, neighbors I think, swarmed the monkeybar house. The girls were cleaning and complaining about the noise the boys were making while out on a safari. Julie couldn't see how they could ever trap something for dinner when making all that noise. The lions were sure to hear them coming.

Karen must have decided it was time her new and very unhappy husband went to work because she was ordering him to do something "constructive." She must have tried to kiss him goodbye because I heard him exclaim, "No mushy stuff or I'll quit your dumb game. I'll resign as father. I'm goin' ta work now." Richard stormed away.

At the other end of the playground or jungle or whatever, Richard perched himself on the jungle gym. Like magic he whipped out a coiled tape measure from his pocket. He was the foreman of his own one-man construction crew. Hanging precariously from a rung, he slowly lowered the tape until one end touched the ground. Proudly to himself he said, " Yep, this is exactly how tall this build-ing should be."

The spell was broken when the teacher blew her whistle . . . . When they went in, they left a barren playground with monkey bars and swings.

Jungle gyms, monkey bars, and swings are, of course, only one kind of transformational stimulus. Here are various others, some elabo-rately protracted:

The girls are busy in the basement again. For a week or two at a time my girls make rooms in the basement. They use old sheets, blankets, bedspreads (we keep all these things for just such occa-sions), old curtains and extra material from sewing. They nail, pin, and tie this material together to create walls for their clubhouses. Each child has a section to be made into a room . . . . Wooden boxes, cardboard boxes, old furniture, rugs, suitcases, boards, beer cases are all used for tables, chairs and beds. There is even a picket fence (left over from a little theatre experience) that they use for a door (the gate part opens for the door). They take their books down and lie on their "beds" to read when they are not busy building . . . . This is usually a winter activity . . . . In the summer this same play takes place, making a "house" by clothespinning a blanket to the fence. This doesn't get nearly as elaborate because it has to be taken down each day. They also put boards from the window sill of the bedroom to the fence that is close to the house at that point and then lay a blanket over the boards for a roof and then the boxes, etc., are carried out, along with the dolls.

Two neighbor girls, ages 4 and 5, pretending to be mothers. One was wearing her mother's high heels, with a blanket tied around her waist. The other had on mother's hat as well as a hand-bag in hand. Dolls seemed to serve as children, and such remarks were heard as "Are you hungry?", "She hurt her knee." "Dinner" was cooked in an old pan, with a stick serving as the stirring spoon. Rose petals on our lawn, as well as weeds from various places in our yard served as ingredients for the pan.

Fortunately, this vital practice need not be limited to early child-hood (Stanislavski and Bertrand Russell are among the celebrated writ-ers who acknowledge that adults who lose this power can no longer do creative work).

I arrived home from class one hot day to find that two of my daughters (11 and 14) were having a water balloon fight with a neighbor girl (13). Nancy had just filled a large long balloon with water and was carrying it in both arms. Suddenly she said, "Hey, this feels like a baby!" The other two girls came over to try holding it and agreed with Nancy. They also filled the same type of balloons with water and decided that the towels they had were baby blankets. Diane, my 14 year old, said, "Say, there is a doll buggy down in the basement. I'll get that for our babies." The three girls played for three hours with their balloon babies.

My 13-year-old brother had a bike wash in our driveway. He had friends from all over out washing their bikes. One boy called his rather beat-up hand-me-down bike his James Bond car. He washed the secret panels, the dangerous hubcaps, the changing license plates, and had to be especially careful around the tail lights. He called off the different parts as he washed and went to extremes to show how he would wash them.

My youngest daughter, age 13, yodeling under the shower at the top of her voice and yelling, "I'm Jane, where are you Tarzan?"

My brother Tommy (12 years old) was burning our papers. The wind was blowing and a flaming paper blew high into the sky and floated to the grass. My brother began a wild flamenco dance as he stomped out the blazing paper and grass. He threw his head to one side and snapped his fingers, the right hand above his head, the left hand down by his side. While he was dancing another piece of paper had flown out of the barrel and rested on the grass. This time he took off at breakneck speed and slid into the burning grass as if he were trying to make it to a base before he was out. He picked himself up, took off his (imaginary) cap and took a bow.

My oldest daughter, age 15, doing a chorus girl routine while the stereo emitted some rag-time jazz.

My oldest son, age 14, watching a televised baseball game, without the sound, pretending to be the announcer " . . . And the pitcher takes a long wind-up, throws a fast curve . . . and retires the second batter in a row."

Nevertheless, it appears that early and middle childhood is the most generally prolific time—at any rate, the most expressive and observable time of life. The child can transform himself and everything else with visible ease.

During student teaching I saw one of the children standing on the playground, being very still with his arms outstretched. This particular boy was an unusually aggressive child, so I asked him what he was doing. He said, "Shh, I am being the fir tree, and trees are very quiet things." (This boy was the fir tree in our class play about a fir tree, 2nd grade.)

My niece, Nicole (2½ years old), has been visiting us a few days this summer . . . . Soap suds in the bathtub become birthday cakes as she sings Happy Birthday . . . . At the supper table she had on a new pair of socks and in the middle of supper she said, "Donelda, my new socks are looking at you!"

Kindergarten classroom—afternoon session.
Mixter school—Lincoln Park, Michigan.
During "free choice" period one little boy chose to play with clay. He molded the clay into different shapes and then he put these shapes of clay on his face. He had some trouble getting the clay to stick to his face but finally did manage.

He had a small clay hat on his head. Triangles of clay were on his forehead and were supposed to be eyebrows. He also had a mustache. He couldn't get the clay to stay on his upper lip and so he looped it over his nose.

He got up from his table and walked over to me. With hands in his pockets and rocking on his heels and toes, he said, "Meet Mr. Shrink-Man." (I have no idea who Mr. Shrink-Man is.)

In the second grade a boy came to school wearing sun glasses . . . . When his teacher inquired as to why he was wearing them, he replied, "I'm a Hollywood movie star in disguise."

Ronnie (age 6) pushed a footstool with his head across the living room into the dining room. He then crawled up onto the stool. Kelley (8) and Eddy (9) were playing on the floor and tried to get Ronnie off the stool. When asked why he was on the footstool, he answered, "Because I brought it out here." Ronnie then curled up into a ball and told all the other children that he was the Great Pumpkin and they were his subjects. They were to bow down to him, but Randy (9) wouldn't; he decided to play Snoopy. Randy said that Snoopy bites mailmen and if he can bite mailmen he can bite a pumpkin. Ronnie said he couldn't bite him because pumpkins don't have legs and he had better bow down or he would tell Santa Claus. According to Ronnie, Santa and the Great Pumpkin were good friends and they went around together. Randy knocked Ronnie off the stool. He replaced Ronnie on the footstool and declared that

the Great Pumpkin was dead and Snoopy was going to be king. The footstool was now Snoopy's doghouse with Randy as Snoopy. Kelley became the Red Baron and tried to shoot Snoopy-Randy down, but he said he was bullet proof. The only way to get him down was to knock him off the stool. Kelley said the Red Baron doesn't knock people off stools—he shoots them off.

At this point the children tired of the game and went outside to play Tarzan in the barn.

Two little boys, approximate age 6 and 8, while their mother was shopping. "Let's play dinosaur!" The two were soon down on their hands and knees, engaged in mock battle. "I'll bite your tail!" and "I'll get you with my claws!" were some of the remarks heard.

The boys in my second grade class like to play cars. They line up and call off the names of their favorite cars and play Grand Prix. They rev up their engines and take off. They run around the playground stripping gears and screeching tires. The winner always gives a speech on the performance of his car.

Neighborhood children, ages 3 through 11, pretending to be car drivers while riding their tricycles, bicycles, and wagons. "Beep! Beep!" and "Honk! Honk!" rang through the air almost continuously. Soon one toddler assumed the role of a policeman. She held both arms apart and firmly commanded "Stop!" Then "Go!" sent the line of vehicles going on their way around our court. After a while, I observed one child using a jump rope at the rear of each child's vehicle. He would take the wooden end of the rope, put it on the bottom rear of the vehicle, make a gurgling noise and say, "You're all filled up!"

The other day the children in the neighborhood had about seven boxes lined up along the sidewalk in back of a red wagon. There were about two children on each box and one little boy in the wagon. The children are all around 4, 5, and 6. One boy was walking along by the side of the train collecting tickets. Then he sat down in the wagon; he apparently became the engineer . . . . He had one of the youngest children sitting on the back end of the wagon, and when he got in the wagon to start his train, he turned around to this little boy and said, "Blow." The little boy was the train whistle.

Being told to observe the dramatic play of children has re-opened my eyes to the wonderful world of drama that unfolds in my own house every day. Often I sit in the same room with my children with my thoughts elsewhere and am not aware of what they are saying and doing as they are playing. It was a great experience just to listen and look with no other thoughts but to find out how children play.

Many of the things I observed were things that I have been aware of before—games like bombs away down the clothes chute to make cleaning a room a little more interesting; basketball games in my living room by older boys with no ball, no basket, but lots of jumping and blocking and scoring, the kind of game that makes everyone and anyone a champion.

. . . But this one seemed a little more special. Cable Car—a temporary clothesline across our patio became a cable car to my 10-year-old as he attempted to cross the Indian Ocean. While his feet never left the ground, David lived through a thrilling adventure as he faced high winds, storms, and eventually became stranded in a cable car that would not operate. He called for help, he sent up flares, and impatiently watched for his rescuer in the form of his 9-year-old brother. David shouted encouragement and directions on how to effect the rescue in the safest possible manner. As soon as the rescue was completed and his car was again operable, both boys were off to other parts of the yard for other adventures.

Water, in all of its forms—from puddle to ocean—is a powerful transformational agent.

My 3-year-old, in the bathtub, observing water droplets that have formed on the inside of the tub:
"April! There's April on there! April!"

Why do your fingers wrinkle when you stay in the bathtub too long? This was the question but the observations of sound came so quickly that little time was given to the answers.

Cynthia rubbed her wrinkled fingers together and remarked, "Sounds like sea gulls—crickets. You can make music when your fingers are wet. Sounds like popcorn popping in the pan."

Whenever Bryan takes a bath he takes a paintbrush in the tub and paints the walls with the bubbles from his bath. Sometimes he has to wipe it off because it's the wrong color, etc.

My 2-year-old niece. While she was taking a bath, she took a Mickey Mouse "Soaky" toy out of the tub and put it on the floor. I said, "What's Mickey doing?", and she answered by saying, "Eating six dozen carrots!!"

My youngest son, age 10, with mounds of soap lather on his chin and cheeks while taking a bath, saying, "Ho! Ho! Ho!"

Pooky (3) and her little brother Darphy (2) were standing still in the rain. I was walking by with an umbrella and stopped and asked them what they were doing out in the rain. Pooky said, "We are flowers and we are standing in the rain so we can grow up and be pretty."

Last summer a little 5-year-old girl was making sand castles on a Lake Michigan beach. She was very much absorbed in what she was doing. Her 7-year-old brother came down to see what was holding her interest so long. As he approached, she told him to stop where he was, and not to come any farther or he would fall into the moat. She said that the king of the castle would have to say it was alright before he could enter. She said that she would talk to the king and tell him that he was her brother and ask if he could come to visit the king and the royal family. She did, and he was permitted to enter. After he had talked with the king for some time, he invited him to come and visit him at his castle someday. He then set about to build his own castle in the sand.

I walked along the beach in Florida. After I got past the section of college students I came upon some families. One little boy, about 5 or 6, was building sand houses just out of reach of most of the waves. I stopped to ask him what he was doing. "I'm building, I'm building a whole city. See, there's the houses, and the gas station and the store; we get ice cream over there." A big wave came and washed his city away.

"That's the end of another hard day's work," he said, and walked away.

Two small boys, about 5 or 6, were playing in a mud puddle near our driveway. They were playing with empty pea-pods, pretending that they were boats. At first there were boats of every kind—from sailboats to submarines. Then a great naval battle developed. The boys blew on the pea-pods to make them go faster, backward, and forward. They splashed the water with their hands to create a rough, stormy sea and dropped rocks on each other's ships as bombs to sink them. Then after this war was over, they fished all the sunken ships from the bottom of the mud puddle and started over again.

Several boys were floating boats in a tub of water while two girls were throwing water into the air to make it rain (ages 2½–5).

Much of our family activity in recent weeks has centered around our new pool. We have built human mountains that were washed away by the "tide," turned the pool into a giant Maytag, had races (everybody cheated), had an animal circus, and created giant tidal waves that wiped out the world. All of the above miracles were performed by persons of ages 4 to 35, with as few as four participants and as many as fourteen. However, the following incident involved only two, ages 6 and 9. Props: two diving masks (they hate water in their noses) and two swim fins, one for each mermaid. Setting: the ocean floor.

The dialogue that follows is in bits and pieces, as I was able to catch it. Key: Wendy: W. Elaine: E.

> E: I can stand on my tail! Wendy, watch me. This is how mermaids move. See? See, your body has to wiggle like this.
> W: I KNOW, Elaine! Now watch me. Let's swim like mermaids.
> E: We can, you know, cause we *are* mermaids. We have tails. And we live under the water. And our hair goes wooooooooo, and floats behind us. See? We're beautiful. (W. swims, seemingly ignoring E.)
> W: Look! I'm swimming! . . .
> E: Look at me wiggle, Wendy! See? This is how they do it.
> W: (giggling) Wiggle! Not wiggle, Elaine; that's how they swim.
> E: I know! Watch me, Wendy!
> W: Watch ME!
> (I dove into the pool at this point. Both girls demanded my instant attention.)
> E: Look, Mom, we're mermaids! I can stand on my tail. Look how big I am. That's cause I'm on my tail. Look, Mom, this is how mermaids swim. I can swim like a mermaid.
> W: I can swim like a mermaid too, Aunt Gail. Watch.

I watched, praised, agreed with their assessment of the talents of mermaids, and noted their slightly embarrassed faces. I wasn't welcome anymore. I left . . . . By the time I was out the gate they were once again in the depths of the ocean.

> E: C'mon, Wendy, let's try to sit on our bottoms and have a tea party.
> (Zoom out. Fade.)

A boy and a girl, 5 and 6 years, just tall enough for the four feet section. "You have to swim under the wall to get away from the sharks," he said.

"Here they come," she squealed. And with great haste, they dove under the floats to safety in the shallowest section.

On the beach of Lake Huron with three boys, ages about 7, 9, and 11. "Hey, let's bury Tim," suggested the oldest. In obvious agreement, they dug out a large hole in the sand and buried Tim up to his neck.

"Let's leave him here for the buzzards to eat," again the oldest boy suggested.

"Yeah, and the ants too!" added the little one.

Mike (who is 8) had just learned to swim. As he jumped off the side of the pool and splashed towards me, he said, "I'm Super Fish! I can swim better than anybody. I can see under water, too."

I asked him what Super Fish had that made him special and he said, "A hundred arms, like an octopus." "I can do my school work a hundred times as fast and I can draw a hundred different pictures too," he answered quickly.

There are probably as many interpretations of his answers as there are people to wonder. Is he so proud of his achievement of learning to swim that he sees himself as Super Fish? Could it be that he is unsure of his ability and announcing that he is Super Fish bolsters his confidence in himself? Maybe there is a facet to this I don't see as yet. I know that seeing under water was a reality because he did open his eyes as he swam underwater.

His comment about having arms like an octopus and what he could do with these arms was amazing in the easy and quick way the answer came. A few more questions cross my mind. Does he find school work so unpleasant that he would like to finish faster or is this just a small joke on his part? Is he so filled with ideas that he could draw a hundred pictures or does he envision this as a most pleasant way to spend time? I don't know the answers; probably neither does Mike. Are there any "right" answers or can we only conjecture as to the reason for Super Fish?

Only conjecture! This is a good moment to reemphasize that we cannot pretend—indeed it is dangerous to presume to know the specific reasons, motives, meanings of a child's play, just as we cannot know the innnermost thoughts of any human being, of whatever age. It is a part of wisdom to realize that we can never wholly understand even our own minds and wishes. Patterned, oversimplified analyses of human behavior are inevitably false and sometimes destructive. The individual's particular combination of imitation and invention at a given moment, the mysterious commingling of experiment, memory, observation, wish, must be humbly respected. The child calling himself Super Fish explains that he has "a hundred arms, like an octopus," and that he can "do my school work a hundred times as fast." Does the adult then infer that he hates his school work or loves it? Obviously, we have no right or reason to deduce either from this single episode of play; it is absolutely essential to learn the difficult art of suspending such judgment, of *knowing that we do not know*. We must resist the temptation to give false answers at a time when we are just ready to ask true questions. Once while I was washing dishes, I overheard my daughters playing out an elaborately detailed situation revolving around a fiendish baby sitter. When I asked later (subtly, casually, I thought!) whether they enjoyed staying with Amy or would rather I didn't go out, they were on to me instantly, and answered (amused, tolerant, sensitive to the hazards of parenting), "Oh, that character was modelled from our *imagination*," "Don't worry, Mama!" I felt like the fool that I was; it was one of those precious moments of truth when you realize the need to practice what you preach. They have given me untabulated quantities of such essential moments. "Why don't they consult the children?" mused Pamela (9), disgustedly examining a drugstore packet of "school" Valentines, "They don't know what we like." It is true that if we are interested in children we must look to them and listen to them as a matter of course. And as we pay attention to their play, we must never violate its complexity by presuming to "decode" or oversimplify it.

Indeed, the key to appreciating the diversity of imagining, of transforming in play is to contemplate as many different examples of it as possible. Here, then, are more representative samples from students:

> (Danvers State Institution, Massachusetts) Standing on the lawn, my 12-year-old student, Erwin, came up with the idea that he would like to be an IRT Lexington Avenue subway train. Then he yelled across to a little old woman passing by, "Lady, Lady, will you marry me? I'm strong as a train—I'll give you a thousand babies!"

> Patty ran into the family room, where I was studying, screaming, "Jeffey bit me!" I went into the bedroom to investigate, and found him sitting on top of the dresser, from where he announced, "I'm an alligator and I'll bite her any time she bothers me."

> Leslie is the 3-year-old brother of my fiance. I made a little stuffed doll for him, and when I took it over to their house to give it to him he was asleep. So I put the doll on the pillow, next to Teddy Bear and Pa Bear. (Ma Bear must have been in another part of the house; she was usually with them.) When Leslie woke up he came running into the kitchen with all of his "critters" under his arm. He

said, "This boy 'peared out of my pillow. Teddy Bear heard him trying to get out, so he said, 'Come out, boy,' and he did. He must be
looking for a home." When I asked Les what he would call the doll
he said immediately, "I'll call him Boy With The Tang Hair." (The
hair was orange.)

My 2-year-old was sitting on the floor ripping up paper. When I
asked her what she was making, she answered very abruptly, "Snow!"

At lunch one day, 4-year-old Lisa said, "Mommy, I'd like to tell
you a story." Her eyes grew round as she withdrew into thought,
amazing herself with the thoughts she was making.
"Once upon a time," she began slowly, "there was a . . ." she
paused for anticipation to grow, " . . . a GIANT GRASSHOPPER!
And, his friend OGRE." She considered what she had said, then
hurried on reassuringly, "The Ogre was really nice. He could even
eat candy with the children. The Giant Grasshopper could even
fly!" She flew from her chair to hop and flap about the room.
Back in her chair, settled and prim, she continued . . . "One
day, when the grasshopper was getting kind of big, he turned into
a frog. The Ogre said, (falsetto) 'Oh, dear, my dear Friend Grasshopper is a frog!' So the Ogre was going to change him back, and
he said, 'Giant Grasshopper! Giant Grasshopper!' And he came out
a . . . WITCH!"
Lisa pressed her fingers to her lips for a moment before add-
ing huskily, "And then the Giant Grasshopper's egg hatched and
out came a BABY Giant Grasshopper."
We were both momentarily awestruck by the picture she had
painted.
Then she explained, "Giant Grasshoppers live in Giant
Houses. They can fly, but they have to hop inside their house because it's so tiny." To illustrate her point, she scrunched herself up
and hopped about the room.
"There's another friend," she continued. "He's really big! Bigger than the Giant Grasshopper, even bigger than the GIANT OGRE!
He really has to squiggle down in his house, like this." Lisa became
a compact ball of bounces. "He's a House Giant. He's really used to
houses."
The most striking part of Lisa's story, to me, was her ability
to build to a climactic point, even though she was inventing each
step of the story as she reached it, and, furthermore, to recognize
that point. She knew, when the Giant Grasshopper was turned into
a witch that something momentous had happened, and she made
the most of it, both in tone of voice and in dramatic pause. Her
eyes were shining and inner focused. Her hands were clenched.
She was totally caught up in her own giant creation.

For her, the story was remarkable in both length and continuity. Her fantasies are often difficult to understand from an adult point of view, perhaps because her verbalizations cover only a part of her mental image, and thus sound fragmented.

Lisa's statement that the Ogre is really nice was actually a sensitive reaction to her listener's possible misunderstanding and fear . . . . Also, she seemed for a moment to be afraid of her own fantasy, and to be reassuring herself.

Isn't that the nicest thing about fantasy? That the maker is always in control, the master, the manipulator of his world, and can turn it off if it becomes overwhelming? How many times have each of us used fantasy to put ourselves in control of a domineering boss or a gossipy neighbor? And when the fantasy comes to the disturbing point, can we not change it to something innocuous but equally effective: a pie in the face?

So much of what she is thinking comes out in Lisa's play . . . . The reference to the Baby Grasshopper connects with her current preoccupation with birth and babies, brought about partially by her age and by an impending birth in her best friend's family. Most of her current verbalized fantasies involve adaptations of information she has recently received on this topic. It seems that play thus helps her to internalize new information. The references to transformation are a further illustration of this point. Lisa has discovered the fascination of magic and magicians and witches who can make anything happen just by waving a wand. If only *we* could just wave a wand and change the world! . . . But growing up sometimes means learning to deny our own magical powers.

My room-mate and I again babysat for Matt (age 3). He was supposed to be in bed, but Hallowe'en was just a few days away, and he just had to tell us about his costume. He would be dressed as a kangaroo, and he demonstrated what a kangaroo looks like. "They have big ears and long tails they can sit on. They can lean back and sit on their tails and pick their feet up. They don't need any feet because their tails are so big—as big as me. But the tail on my suit isn't as big because I'm just a baby. The big kangaroos are bigger than my daddy. They jump like this, but I can't jump big like they do. They can go across the room in one jump, but it takes me nine or seven." Matt really got involved in this demonstration. "Kangaroos have pockets right here," (pointing to his stomach) "and theirs have babies but mine will have candy because I'm too little to have a baby." He told us that he had tried to get his mother to let him put his baby sister in his pocket, but she had convinced him that Tracy was too big.

(Trying on my swimming cap one last time before bed.)

> *Amina (3½):*   I'm a spaceman.
> *Mama:*   Where are you going?
> *Amina:*   To the moon.

I stopped to see my aunt and caught her in the middle of her house cleaning. I was there about 15 minutes when we heard the vacuum start. In the middle of the living room floor my 7-year-old cousin was playing space ship. He sat on the vacuum yelling orders into the hose. "More speed, we must get to Mars. We must save those people. Mars men have four heads and big mouths and like to eat earth people. Billy, Billy! Watch out! We're gonna hit the moon. Whew, that was close. Those Mars people stole our earth guys. We got to save 'em. Billy, get into your space suit. I'll land this ship." After a few minutes of "landing," he turned off the vacuum and crawled into his bedroom, checking behind each table and chair on his way.

This one has to be seen to be appreciated. Both girls (2 and 3-years-old) were marching around the house the other night playing tom toms, dressed in shorty pajamas, white boots (not snapped), and wearing their dolls' green and red underpants on top of their heads.

I was caring for a 4-year-old girl while her parents were out for the evening. I went to put her to bed and say goodnight to her, and as I was pulling the drapes closed, she asked me not to close them because she liked to sleep with them open because sometimes, she would hear faeries singing outside the window. She loved to listen to their songs. The music that they made was so soft that she could hardly hear it. It made her feel good and then she would get very sleepy and would fall asleep.

The boys and girls in my second grade class found many uses for crepe paper strips. At recess many of them picked up the strips which I had left on the table and ran outside. One boy was a jet with a vapor trail behind. Another was a weather man and climbed the jungle gym and let it fly to see which way the wind was from. Five girls tied them around their waists and became members of a secret club.

They were on an oil drum in the yard next door. Dennis, the captain, was yelling orders: "Batten down the hatches! Lower the sails!" They rocked the oil drum so hard that Steven fell off. The next thing I heard was, "Man overboard! Get a rope!" Tracy ran into his house and got a rope. While Tracy was gone Dennis screamed, "Sharks!" Up to this point Steven, the man overboard, was just sitting on the ground watching, but when he heard "sharks" he stood up and started running around, moving his arms in a swimming motion. Dennis called to Tracy to hurry up with the rope, and about three minutes later, Tracy appeared with a six-foot piece of string and a piece of peanut butter and jelly bread. Dennis took the rope in a very disgusted manner and threw it to Steven, who was reeled in and back on the ship in a matter of seconds.

There was one more person on the ship—Teresa, who up to this point had just held on, trying to keep herself on the ship . . . . Now she screamed out, "Look, Steven's leg is cut." At first everyone believed her, including me, until we all glanced at both of Steven's legs. Dennis went right along with her and said "Probably was one of the sharks." Teresa grabbed a rag and began wrapping Steven's leg. Tracy's mother now appeared and asked to see Steven's leg. When she found out that he was not actually hurt, she called them all in for lunch.

There were two little boys about 4 lying on the pant rack under the pants, looking up. "Hey Joe hand me the wrench." "Okay." They were fixing a car.

Three children, an 8-year-old girl, a 5-year-old boy and an 11-year-old boy were playing with an older brother's tape recorder. They had just landed on the moon in their space ship and were interviewing some of the moon maids and moon men, to find out about life on the moon. I watched as they played out the action, and then saw their excitement as they played back the recording and heard their own voices. As they landed on the moon, there was the sound of the spaceship—various beeping noises, and then there was the sound of the door slamming on the ship as they went out. Then their actual interviews with the moon people. They described the moon people as being only two feet tall, with bushy red hair, and wide, ear-to-ear grins on their faces. Their eyes glowed in the dark and their ears were like mouse ears, and their feet had very large toes. When they walked, they waddled like ducks and when they spoke, it sounded like the three chipmunks speaking "Pig Latin." They talked to them and drank some "Moonshine" with them and then returned to their spaceship and blasted off for the Earth.

Amina (3½), playing with a piece of braided plastic lace and hearing the noise it makes when pulled and twisted: "There are bees in there."

A little girl of 4, with whom I am very well acquainted, told me a beautiful story that revealed the depths of her imagination. We were sitting together on her bed, and I had been trying to get her to sleep. However, her mind was on the animals that live in the darkness under the bed. She told me to be very quiet and listen, because the alligator was coming. I expressed surprise, and she told me not to be afraid; it was a friendly alligator. She put her hand under the head-board and reached down to stroke him. "Hi, little alligator (he's only a baby one). Do you want to pet him?" I asked if he would bite me. "No," she said, "he doesn't have his teeth in yet." I waited until she asked him if it was O.K. for me to pet him; then I reached down to do it, after she had told me, "He says it's O.K. if you're gentle."

. . . And then they became "beautiful young maidens" whose beaus had just given them bouquets of "sun flowers sprinkled with stardust."

Two boys, approximately 6 and 7 years old, walking down the street, gazing around them; the older turned to the other and said, "Boy, if all this snow was ice cream, cows would really be out of business!"

Two little girls raking leaves decided to play house, with the leaves serving as room divisions. They designed an elaborate floor plan, and played—for a long time—inside their leaf house.

I watched three boys and two girls playing with a big cardboard box. Within a half hour that box served as a prison, a train, a doghouse, and a people house. They assumed changing roles with little discussion; for example, "I know! It's a doghouse." And everyone became dogs that quickly. When they were through with the box, they broke it all down flat and lay down on it, "sleeping."

The day before yesterday I was walking past the playground of Roosevelt School, and two boys (about 6 years old) peeked around from the side of a big tree. One said, "I am a fiery dragon and I'm going to eat you up!" Then he exhaled very forcefully, and because it was a chilly day, his breath really did look smoky.

My two sons, ages 10 and 14, sent out to take garbage cans back to their proper place, using the lids as shields and their extended arms as swords.

My 3½-year-old, jumping off a low stool, arms stretched sideward: "My wings are SO excited!"

The deaf children in Rackham School play that they are

crippled by using ladders and crutches and a wagon for a wheelchair.

I walked home from school one day with four children who live three houses down from me. As we came around the corner we saw that their yard was all dug up (drainage problem). Suddenly Mary exclaimed, "They're digging for hidden pearls." I asked, "What pearls?" "Why, the pearls our street is named after."

It was a beautiful day today, and as I sat watching the children on the playground at Roosevelt School, I overheard three boys (about age 8) talking. "Hey, I found gold!" shouted one, as he stooped over to pick up a muddy rock. "Yeah? Let's look for more," replied the second boy, as he ran off to the swings to explore the ground there.
I watched them hunt all over . . . . They would scoop up a handful and let some of the pebbles sift through so they could find the "gold." They found quite a lot; their pockets were bulging.
I guess it takes a child to see gold in ordinary mud and dirt. It's never "ordinary" to them!

Manifestly, play indeed "transcends the immediate needs of life," as Huizinga puts it, and "confirms the supra-logical nature of the human situation."

CHAPTER FOUR

To Master Reality

Amina (3½):   Hey, where's Amina?
Mama: In bed.
Amina: What's she doing?
Mama: Probably dreaming.
Amina: I'd better go check her. (She walks up some imaginary stairs. Coming back:) She's not dreaming.
Mama: How do you know?
Amina: She's just closing her eyes so she can't see the dream.

For the young child, the waking dream of the real world—as perceived by the conscious mind—is still amazing, even fantastic; and the sleeping dream—woven by the unconscious—can be as real as the realm of daylight. "The impossible and the possible mingle," says Hazard, "the conscious does not differ from the subconscious. . . . Everything is real, nothing is real." This mental fluidity—a state optimally conducive to learning, invention, and discovery—is mystifying and even alarming to those adults who have fixed their own minds in rigid patterns grown necessary to their own comfort and safety. Some of these claim that they do not dream at night, or at most, immediately lose, forget their dreams at the instant of waking; some say that they cannot remember any of their childhood experiences; some insist that they are entirely governed by reason, purely rational thought; or that intuition is always "women's."

Such people are inclined to shut children—even their "own"—out of their lives; they are afraid of a child's mind. For instance, a worried woman told me that the family dinner that evening had been turned into a catastrophe because their 6-year-old son had asked if there was a hole in the bottom of the ocean. Her husband had flown into a rage, had told the child "no," asked him what was wrong with him to make him get such crazy ideas, and had left the table without finishing his meal. The woman timidly asked, "What about a question like that? *Is* it crazy?—or is it O.K.?" It seems more reasonable to ask why a child should *not* inquire about the bottom of the ocean. How, after all, is he to find out things he does not know? Maybe he heard the song somewhere; if so, to be struck by so captivating an image is natural. He may have been entertaining ideas of connections (there *is* a hole in that most familiar body of water, the bathtub), trying to perceive some grand design in the world. The scientists who first saw the parallel order between submicroscopic structures and galaxies probably asked such questions as children.

What is important to understand is that child's play (including the imaginative mental play which comes out through words, like the ocean-hole question), however fantastic it may be, is *not* ultimately *escape* from, but a *bridge* to reality. "When a child has started to *play* with some newly acquired component of understanding," says Kornei Chukovsky, in *From Two To Five*, ". . . he has become full master of this item of understanding." To say "full master" seems extravagant, but most authorities agree that *the essential aim of play is to master reality.* And, in absorbing that idea, it is necessary always to remember that play and reality are both infinitely more complex than they are sometimes assumed to be.

Turning again to the children themselves, as seen through the students' eyes, here are a variety of samples of the child's imaginative efforts to connect aspiration and possibility, later with now, the known with the unknown, legend and life:

> When I was student teaching (second grade) we saw a movie about Johnny Appleseed. The next day one of the little boys came to school with an old pot on his head. How he got it to school I don't know. But he informed me of his new identity and that he was going out to plant apple trees. I asked him when he was going to do this. His reply: "At recess."

> I sometimes babysit for 5-year-old Bobby. Last summer he gave me a ten-cent ring and asked me to marry him. I asked him how old he was going to be when I married him. He said that he'd be "old enough to have a paper route so he could have money for us."

> It happened one weekend while I was taking care of my cousin, who is 5. I must inject the fact that my father is a minister. Chris was in his bedroom playing by himself. I went in to see what

he was doing and there he was with a Bible in one hand and a bowl full of change in the other hand. I asked him what he was doing and he said, "I'm practicing to be like Uncle Herb. Then I can have lots of money. Cause Uncle Herb gets to keep all those bowls of money that the men pass around." Well, I tried to explain that the money was for the church and not for Uncle Herb. He just looked at me in wonder. The next day in church when the collection plate was passed, Chris slowly dropped in five of his ten pennies and said, "That's for the church and the rest is for Uncle Herb." When we walked out of church, Chris went over to my father and said, "Uncle Herb I think you could use this." (Chris has decided not to become a minister.)

While walking down the street on a warm afternoon, I passed two boys around 10 years of age. One was walking and the other had a crash helmet on and was riding a bicycle. The latter said to the first, "You know, I think I'll major in demolition derby and old stock cars."

Play is triggered in any place at any time; like actors studying plot and character, children conjecture randomly about human actions and motivations.

Over Thanksgiving vacation my fiancé and I took his two nephews to Howard Johnson's for a milk shake. (Randy is 7 and Billy is 5.) Because we weren't ordering very much, we sat at the counter. The only other person at the counter was an old man, sitting five seats away.

As we were drinking our shakes we all noticed the man pull out a pen from his shirt pocket and write something about two or three lines long, on his place mat. He then slowly tore that section off from the place mat and folded the small paper in half. He put the pen back in his pocket but he kept the paper in hand while he slowly continued drinking his coffee. (He was still doing this as we left.)

As soon as Randy and Billy saw this man folding his paper, they both started suggesting things that the man could have been writing:

Randy: He's got a ransom note to give to the manager.

Billy: He's figuring his bill.

Randy: He drew a floor plan for a robber.

Billy: He just remembered someone's phone number.

Randy: He wrote down a secret formula to pass on to another spy who is coming.

Billy: He's asking the waitress for a date.

Randy: Someone's following him and he wants the waitress to call the police.

Billy: He's afraid to tell the waitress he hasn't got any money.

This continued even after we left. The final suggestions that the boys offered came several hours later as we were leaving their home. (I really wouldn't be surprised if even today they still wonder just what that man wrote!):

Randy: He wrote a hold-up note.
Billy: He was afraid to ask the waitress out loud where the bathroom was.

Anne (5) is an only child and there are no other children in the neighborhood. Anne has an imaginary friend who lives in the kitchen under the stove. On one occasion when I was babysitting for Anne, I was amazed at how long she played with her friend. It was as if she actually had a playmate with her. She played dolls and had a tea party with her imaginary friend. Later, her mother and I talked about Anne and her friend, and she said that this had been going on for almost five months. Every day Anne gets down by the stove and gets her friend out, and off they go to play together. Several weeks later I asked Anne how her friend was and she nonchalantly replied, "We had a fight and I sent her away." I found out later from her mother that a few days before, a new family moved in next door and that they had a little girl about Anne's age. Now Anne has made a new friend, but I think that one of these days Anne will be down on the floor looking under the stove for her old friend.

It is quite possible that Anne will look for her imaginary friend again; it is also possible that she may not. What is certain is that Anne was imaginatively practicing human relationships—in order to be readier—until some real children happened along to play.

Mark, 10, was convinced that he was an engineer. He carried a ball of string and a box of modeling clay with him at all times. He would rig up systems of wires and inventions with these simple tools. He could explain the workings of some appliances which he hadn't invented yet. At recess one day he was taken to see a movie based on the Homer Price series, which involved a doughnut machine that could not be stopped. Mark sat quietly for a while as the picture progressed and the characters kept trying to fix the switch. Soon he began to wiggle, and finally when he could contain himself no longer, he shouted out, "For heaven's sake, pull out the plug on the silly machine!"

One night at the restaurant where I work, I started talking to a little boy, about 8 years old. I had noticed him eating green onions with a hot fudge sundae. We just chatted generally at first, and finally I asked him if he liked onions with ice cream, and if he did, to tell me so I could try it. He suddenly informed me he was a scientist and eating onions and ice cream was an experiment, and if I wanted to know how it tasted, I would have to read the "article" he was going to write about it.

Through this serious playing at house, I learned much and identified myself as being a wife and mother. I was playing, but at the same time I was seriously preparing myself for when I would grow up. I know that I played at being a mother many more times than at being a wife. Perhaps this is why I now feel more capable of being a mother than of being a wife.

Even going to bed and sleeping are practiced through playing:

When babysitting with a 3-year-old girl, I went in to check whether she was sleeping, because I had put her in bed to take a nap. She had taken all of her clothes out of her dresser and piled them on the floor, and she was lying down in the second drawer. I said to her, "I thought you were supposed to be in bed sleeping," and she said in a determined and disgusted tone, "I am in bed and I am sleeping." So I didn't say any more. I just left her there. And when I went back after a few minutes, she had put her clothes back and was asleep in bed.

My niece, Kari, age 2 years, remembers vividly what "no" means; however, she can't resist playing with the piano keys. She plays the piano with one hand and slaps it with the other hand, while saying to herself, "No! No! No!"

5-year-old spanking male and female figurines, "Naughty mommy, naughty daddy, I don't ever want to see you again!"

Mike, 6½, being informative: "If you lock a monster in a room you shouldn't have anything valuable in it, like a vase or anything—just a plain ole room, without anything in it, cause they'd break it for sure."
Watching a scene on t.v. he asked: "I'd walk behind a robot, wouldn't you?" Why? "Because," Mike continued, "when we catch boys over in the field, we walk behind them so they can't do any tricks to us."
Figuring out what to do with the captured girls in a planned game: "Maybe we could put them in a hollow tree—but there's lots of 'em. Two big ones (in the third grade), one in the second, and in the first and two in *no* grade. They'd never all fit!"

As in such great fantasies as Tolkien's Ring Trilogy, child's play is intricately realistic within the framework of its assumptions. Imitation and imagination combine in the ongoing attempt to penetrate and master reality.

Repetition as a Means of Absorbing New Knowledge and Experience

This is a composition written by a third grade boy, entitled *My Brain:*

> It's like this—if you rob a bank and you do it over and over and over and over and over and over and over and over and over and over and over you'll think that it is right to rob a bank.

What a vivid example of the artistic principle that form and content must be unified!

Beyond that, this one-sentence theme by an author that Hemingway would surely have admired expresses a general truth found in studying child's play: that *repetition* is used as a means of learning life. Through repetition, the child ritualizes and exalts what he needs and desires to do, such as eating:

> Kevin, our 21-month-old grandson, with complete absorption and evident delight, makes believe dipping up imaginary food and feeding himself and me. Then the last time he visited us he added a new bit to the routine. He fed himself and his grandfather ("Bapa" is what he calls him) and then after they have both "eaten" they must whack their stomachs and say, "full, full." This game can go on for as long as the grownups can hold up.

A lot has been written on the matter of concentration spans of different ages, but in many such situations as the above, the child's endurance appears to outlast the adult's to as yet unmeasured degrees.

Through repetition, the child may work to prepare for a new and strange event—whether welcomed, feared, or both:

> Sheri is my 3-year-old granddaughter. She is very excited these days about the baby. Ever since her mother said that they were going to get a new baby at their house, she talks about it all the time. Sheri was playing with her doll house. She was talking to herself, just audibly, while arranging the doll house furniture: "This one is for Mommy, this one is for me, this one is for Baby." She remained at play for several moments, repeating all of this; then she suddenly yelled, "Where's our baby now?"

My 10-year-old sister and two younger cousins were playing in the swimming pool. . . . I was in the front yard when I heard screaming: "My god, my god!" I raced to the pool, and there they were playing. One was the life guard, and the other two took turns "drowning." When one was "drowned out" she traded places with the life guard. . . . Over and over they played the different roles. They thrashed and cried, playing their roles as if they had been through the experience before. It was so natural! When they were tired of it, they just quit. They didn't have to talk about it or tell anyone "Today I pretended I was drowning!" It was a release. Maybe it was something that they wanted to make real for themselves. What *is* it like? How *does* it feel?

And in their own way, they experience, they feel, they see, they act and react.

Perry Pre-school
Ricky (4) is very close to his mother, and when she began working for the first time he was upset at the separation. He found a way of regaining his security and adjusting to the change. Ricky would dress in heels, orange skirt, shawl, and hat. Taking a purse, he would be Mrs. Ricky for most of the day. The little boys are masculine oriented, and I have never seen one dress up as Ricky did. It was done with great care and deliberation. For two weeks Ricky was Mrs. Ricky every day. He went shopping, made cupcakes, and went to work. Gradually he spent less and less time as Mrs. R., finally discarding all his finery for a teeter-totter ride. While Ricky was dressed up he was not taunted, berated, or ridiculed by any of the children. This was surprising because the boys wouldn't hesitate to laugh at any behavior considered unmanly. Perhaps they followed the example of the teachers. Perhaps they recognized a need. Perhaps they were too wrapped up in their own concerns to bother with Ricky until he wanted to bother with them. I wish I knew.

Piaget has said that play helps the child to assimilate experience. "Through play, more than anything else, the child achieves mastery of the external world," says Dr. Bruno Bettelheim:

> . . . He learns to deal with his psychological problems as he re-enacts in play the difficulties he has encountered in reality . . . he repeats again and again in his play any event that has made a great impression on him in reality. Through repetition he tries to become familiar with it.

The episodes above also reveal the child at play as a primitive, working sympathetic magic. When Ricky enters into the being and function of the mother, he psychologically gains power; he achieves a mea-

sure of control over the circumstances of his life. Instead of being help-
less and passive, he becomes—by dramatic representation—the active
agent. Surely there is a parallel between this and the Cheyenne Indian
dressed in the buffalo robe for the sacred ritual dance conceived to
identify him with the creature most essential to his survival. The Sen-
eca priest wearing the godmask takes on the power necessary to exor-
cise evil and danger from the village; he can, in fact—believing in his
own powers and communicating that faith—restore the spirits of a sick
person, thereby summoning up the patient's will to recover (a factor in
curing which is now generally recognized by modern medicine). The
girls repeatedly playing at drowning were performing a related kind of
primitive magic ritual: by reenacting the feared form of death, they
were making themselves safe from the reality. They imaginatively "experienced" and again and again "survived" drowning; and it is worth
noting that by playing thus freely in the water they were at the same
time actually, physically becoming safer from drowning by increasing
their comfort and skill in the water. It makes sense to me to compare
this kind of dramatic play to the principle and workings of vaccination:
by voluntarily introducing a controlled sample of the danger into one-
self, one's being absorbs the necessary degree of that feared force and
(a true natural marvel) is thereupon strengthened against it. It becomes possible to live with the peril, and to cope with the fear of it: a
reaching toward the mastery of reality.

Belief in magic and marvels is not embarrassing to young children, who are—as already suggested—inclined to be naive and unself-
conscious about invoking supernatural forces by means of their
dramatic imaginations. Like Huckleberry and Tom, some children are
still willing to try charms and seek connections with whatever powers
may occur to them:

> Robert is 10 and Robbie is 7½. They deliver the paper to the
> house I live in. One day I was leaving just as they had delivered the
> paper. I said "hi" and began walking with them, when Robbie re-
> minded Robert of "the curse." Naturally I asked what "the curse"
> was and after some hesitation and some discussion as to who
> would tell me, they decided that if I waited while they delivered
> their last paper, they would tell me. So it was on the corner in front
> of that apartment building that I found out what the horrible
> "curse" was, after, of course, they had assured me that it was a real
> curse because they didn't make it up, they heard it from a friend of
> theirs. The idea is that if a friend sees you walking with a girl it is his
> duty to go up to you, take the little finger of your left hand and wrap

the little finger of his left hand around it, and say solemnly, "Pick a number from 1 to 10," which you must do. Then he says, "Which do you like better: days, weeks, centuries or years?" (in that order), and you must pick one. Finally, he says "For the next six centuries (or whatever number or time period you choose) you must say 'I love you' to every girl you meet." After cautioning me again on the validity of the ritual, Robbie assured me that it happened to him and he has to do it for the next seven years (and proving it, disappearing down an alley with the approach of his student teacher). Then, much to the relief of all of us, deciding that I wasn't to be counted as a real girl, they invited me to have a Coke with them at Ted's.

While walking through the hall, the 8-year-old made up a game to "Don't Step on a Crack." The hall has a floor of black and white tiles, and he made up the game of "Don't step on a white square or you'll marry Betty_____tomorrow." I inquired about "Betty_____" and discovered that "she was the ugliest girl in the world," and was in his class.

Sometimes, as they begin to learn that their culture considers such ideas "childish"—foolish and ignorant, that is—children continue to fill such needs under the protective guise of "kidding" (a word which in itself reveals our society's condescending attitudes toward the young). Adults continue this practice with charm bracelets, horoscopes, wood-knocking: necessary outlets for an ancient, deep sense that there in fact may be more in heaven and earth than is dreamed of in our philosophy. But most of them disclaim these feelings. Only the most sophisticated and the most naive minds can acknowledge that the mysteries of the universe are more complex than we can understand— let alone control—and that we therefore need not, ought not to pretend that all is known and commonplace. The child and the wise adult frankly wonder. But between true childhood and true maturity is a long gap, during which suppression of wonder shrinks the mind's dimensions. The child on the brink of that period sometimes clings to his curiosity and aspirations in wonderfully devious ways. Here for example, are two letters written by second graders in fulfillment of an assignment in the forms of letter-writing:

Kaiser School
April 21, 1967

Dear, good Rainbow Fairy,
    Please tell the clouds to stop raining. We want to go outside and play.

We think that you wear pretty clothes. Please make us pretty dresses like yours. Will you make us pretty like you are?

We want to know if a person can walk across the rainbow. It looks like a bridge. Do you use special shoes to walk on it?

We want to know why you sometimes live in mud puddles and in where the water comes out of the hose.

Do you have any bad fairies or witches for friends? Shame on you if you do.

Love,
Marguerite, Tammy, Diana

A straightforward request for controlled elements (favorable to the desired play), beauty, technical know-how, pure knowledge, and a character reference (reassurance on the existence of absolute good). In the prescribed letter-writing form! The fascination of evil is also present in the second grade:

Dear Witch,

I would like if you would tell me where you live. I may want to come over some day. Can I see your pots and pans and can I taste your brew. And stay a day.

If just we can play a magic game and feed the bats and fly on the brooms. When can I come?

Your friend,
Darlene

This one was addressed to "The Street Where You Live." Somehow the tone is both authoritative and entreating; there are no question marks in the first paragraph, which looks more like demand. Only the time is a question, and the magic playing, batfeeding, and flying are wishes. The child can say that she does not really believe any of this; instead she is now using art to express these thoughts and feelings.

One of my cherished possessions is a 2" x 3" booklet, crudely made of rough brown paper toweling from the school lavatory, with black bats and *Spell Appointment Book* purple-lettered on the cover. On the flyleaf: THIS BOOK BELONGS TO *Winifred Witch* (the name is, of course, in Winifred's handwriting). Twenty small pages follow, such as:

Potions
Thursday Nov. 13
3:40 P.M.
Mix up sickness solution, let out in Princess Agnes' room
Object: something to do

Potions
Monday April 19
10:00 P.M.
Mix up a poisonous potion and dip apple in it—give apple to
princess
Object: publicity

Potions
Friday March 20
9:30 A.M.
Poison King Kuwait and his son with the agony potion
Object: revenge

Potions
Friday *Dec. 25*
All Day
Mix potion to put myself to sleep all day
Object: not wanting to hear the festivities

Potions
Thursday June 11
1:30 A.M.
Mix potion and turn one whole sixth grade into pink pieces of
paper
Object: fun

Other "Potion" pages, consistently following the same form, include
"Mix up an invisible potion, drink it, go to Princess Anne's christening,
and jinx her—Reason: nothing to do;" and "Fly around on broom, dropping plant-killing potion on all vegetation —Object: meanness." (This
last great plague plan was scheduled for November, with winter on her
side!) There were also pages under the casual label of "Just Wickedness"
and "Transformation": e.g., "Every day, any time—Fly around and turn at
least five people into stone—Object: Daily exercise;" "Turn Ambrose into
a toad and try out a little blue cat potion on someone—Object: experiment." Six pages are headed "Kidnapping": e.g., an October entry sched-
uling "capture of Harvest Goddess so there will be no harvest;" "Capture
lovely princess and lock her in tower—Object: added atmosphere for
house;" and "Kidnap handsome prince—Object: marriage." Under "Commonplace Spells": "Place poison spindles where princesses can prick
themselves—Object: tradition." This booklet—written during math
class, it turned out, by my 11-year-old daughter Pamela—exemplifies
combinatorial dramatic play on paper, carried on privately for the pure

exploratory joy of drawing together and rearranging elements from life and literature into a unique new unit. The humor is an essential leavening agent in the material, which does deal with pervasive evil powers needing to be brought under control in some way. (Hughes Mearns, in *Creative Power,* describes this kind of free play and art which goes on "underground" in school as the best release of imagination generally available to older children in our society.) The magical rite as an experiment in psychological power continues to be an element of dramatic play as the developing child makes the transition into art—what Von Lange calls "the mature form of play."

Dramatic Imagination as Practical Rationalization

Another way in which the child's playing functions is very utilitarian, and becomes the mental craft of adult rationalization.

At the supermarket, a boy of about 3 years of age was actively engaged in conversation with his mother. When her attention turned to her shopping, the boy discovered a spray can of deodorant. After examining the can for some time, he placed the cap on his ear, and using the can as the mouthpiece, he carried on a great phone conversation with his grandmother. He told her about the various things he had looked at in the store and which ones he thought he would like to have. At the conclusion, he returned to his mother, and informed her that he had talked to Grandma on the telephone and she felt that he should have some magnets.

. . . My tutoring session with Helen (6) was a running stream of her talk, so I finally mentioned that she had better get busy with her numbers. She sighed, and said, "My mouth gets so dry when I don't talk, I just have to keep talking."

In Flint one of the city parks has an area called Safetyville. It is a miniature driving practice area for young children. Stop signs, lights, railroad tracks, and roads are parts of the scene. Each child drives a small pedal car around the roads, obeying the traffic signals.

One child visiting Safetyville was very excited. She was all set in her open bottom car when she had a toilet accident. The situation was evident to all. Not to be caught responsible, the child called the officer over and—pointing to the wet spot—said, "Hey, this car is leaking gas."

That, as the old joke goes, is savoir-faire. Another way of mastering reality!

Ceremonies of Dark Old Children

Another part of reality, another kind of magic rite which children practice through their play is the ceremonial rituals of the society in which they find themselves:

> Also . . . one of the children in the class (second grade) had read about a "christening" and wanted to know if we could christen our rocket and give it a name. I agreed, and the children planned the whole "christening," complete with a committee and a speech naming the ship. Then the whole class toasted the rocket with Kool-Ade.

> I visited a friend last week and accepted their 5-year-old's invitation to a play wedding. He and his sister were getting married and somebody "had to be the marrier": me. (My friend told me later that they do this all the time, ever since their cousin had got married, and Kathy was flower girl and Tommy ring-bearer.)
> I started to say, "We are gathered here . . . " but was abruptly halted by Tommy, who said I would "have to do it our way—we made all the plans and it has to go the right way."
> He then gave me the lines he wanted, so I learned them and began again. "I marry Tommy to Kathy to live in a big house and have four kids." That was that. Tommy refused to kiss the bride when Kathy said it was time.

Some weddings are more elaborate—and more urgent.

> My boyfriend's niece and all of her friends from the neighborhood had a wedding for their two cats. Gwen is 8, and most of the other children involved were about that age, also.
> First of all, they went all out to make a bow tie for Charky (the male cat) and some flowers for the bride (which they hung around her neck). They made an altar out of a box and a veil for the bride. They even found a ring to fit the bride. After everything was decorated they paraded around the yard to the imaginary church. They sang, "Here comes the bride," as they marched the bride to the altar. They read from the Bible and went through the wedding vows quite accurately. Then they put the two cats in a decorated wagon and paraded the neighborhood. The cats were quite good through the whole thing; they just submitted and let the kids have their fun.
> After it was all over I was talking to Gwen about it, and I asked her why they had a wedding for Charky. She said, "Because the girl cat is going to have kittens and I think Charky is the father, so they had to get married right away."

To Master Reality

·   65

In *The Games of Children,* Bett writes that "some anthropologists
. . . explain many of the rites accompanying marriage . . . as magical ceremonies. . . . A wedding is a rite of passage, and to enter into a new condition or indeed to do anything for the first time is always considered
as attended with supernatural dangers." Another "rite of passage" is
the funeral ceremony, which functions to observe the transition from
life to death, or from this world to another. Children practice this ritual
as well, sometimes in conjunction with the actual burial of a bird, a
turtle, a goldfish (with truly loved pets such as dogs, burial is likely to
be not play or practice, but genuine mourning).

> *Me:* Oh look! Your cat has killed another bird!
> *Jo:* Dad, Dad—come and take the bird from Blackie's mouth!
> *Me:* Let's bury it, O.K.?
> *Jo:* Yeah—wait till I call Sandy and Judy.

We all set to work. Two build a coffin and two make a cross.
A piece of satin is found for the inside of the coffin. We place the
bird in the box and nail the lid on. I lead the procession to the old
oak tree where numerous other birds, turtles, etc. are buried. Jo is
last because she is going to say the prayers over the bird. Sandy
digs a hole. The bird is placed in it. Jo says a prayer. Judy covers
the box with dirt. We cry. Jo says another prayer. She asks that
Blackie be forgiven for killing the bird and also pleads that he be
helped to be a better cat.

We all march back into the house with heads bowed and sit
quietly for a minute. Then back to playing.

Sometimes the children themselves play out death:

Two 6-year-olds were carrying a third very carefully, remind-
ing each other that the patient was in terrible condition and if they
dropped her she would die. They set her down, patted her head,
and took her pulse. Another boy came running up with a stick to
examine her and shook his head: "She's going to die; *don't let her
know.*" Very seriously they sat by until she dramatically sighed and
gave her last breath. They pronounced her dead and covered her
with her own flared skirt.

Walking away, the sad party dried their eyes and all were si-
lent as they sat down on their sidewalk home. Impatiently, the
body moved and peeked out from behind the yellow skirt. The
"doctor" hurried over and yelled, "A ghost, a ghost, run every-

body!" They all got up and ran, including the corpse. Everyone laughed and they played on the swings.

Death and *resurrection!* The immortal spirit rises to play and swing again. Whole books are devoted to this subject, too. The essence is that it is difficult—some claim impossible—for children to believe in or even conceive of permanent death. (And no one has yet been able to prove them wrong.)

Catharsis

Aristotle, in defining tragedy, says that its incidents must arouse "pity and fear wherewith to accomplish its catharsis of such emotions." Clearly, one of the functions of the child's dramatic play is to purge him of strong feelings—anxieties over loss and separation, over pride, identity, relations with other people and with the elements, death, birth, mating. The accumulated examples already given here are rich with emotion which, if bottled up instead of played out, would become dangerous to the child. It should be remarked also—for the sake of balance and truth—that among the feelings which burst to be released through child's play are love, celebration, and joy. The experiencing and the expressing of the whole spectrum of human passions is one essential aspect of the all-encompassing purpose of play: *to master reality.*

CHAPTER FIVE

....

Flow and Form

One of the most powerful exercises in mastering reality through the dramatic imagination comes in the form of *projected play*. When the child builds whole cities and kingdoms, combining blocks, tinker-toys, miniature figures of people, cars, airplanes, ships, etc., he identifies with each and all of these characters and forces, transcending any one and projecting his emotions, his thoughts, his will into the whole complex unit. In effect, he practices the power of head of the family or chairman of the board, of tribal chief or president of a nation or king of an empire—even (since his control extends to the inner thoughts and inter-actions in his creation) a god-like power. This form of dramatic play, carried out sometimes alone and sometimes in collaboration with one or more other children, can be extremely complicated, and often extends over several hours for one session. It is a kind of playing which the child will sometimes need to carry over into a series of sessions; the wish and need to save the arrangement of buildings, props, objects, or figures representing characters, so that the playing can be further elaborated, continued from where it left off (interrupted by meals, sleep, and other such necessities more often than by loss of interest) should be respected when space allows. Clearly, this sort of practice prepares the player not only for such occupations as architecture, engineering, city planning, and scene design, but also for parenting, law, social work, governing. And at a deeper level, the child experiments with relationships and values in intricate ways. It is significant that the Museum of Childhood in Edinburgh, Scotland, now exhibits a Barbie doll and others of her category (including male figures); the museum's scholars and curators recognize the vital place in child development of miniature *adult* doll-figures into which the player's thoughts, feelings, actions can be projected. They occupy a respected place, along with the life-sized baby dolls so vital to other forms of play.

But it is essential to remember that *any* materials (symbolically transformed) can be used in projected play:

Hawkins Elementary School
Brighton, Michigan,
Thursday, October 24, 1974
Fifth Grade—Recess
Sand on the playground, twigs, a piece of gum wrapper, tiny stones, two girls (10 years old):

A: This is the living room, and these lines are where the bedrooms are.

B: You only need one bedroom for a honeymoon house.

A: Mine has two in case somebody comes to visit.

B: OK.

A: See, here's the little lake down here, and I'm going to make these stones be the bench where Kevin and Diane can sit and look at the water.

B: Where's the dock, so they can go swimming?

A: They're just going to sit here . . . see, this stone is Kevin and this one is Diane.

B: Hey, I'm the neighbor on the next hill. Let's connect our roads so we don't have to repair two roads.

A: OK, but they're already up my road, and their car is stuck, but they don't care 'cause they're not going to use it for awhile . . . see this long stone is their new red car.

B: This is the fireplace in my living room. [another stone]

A: Oh, yeh, I better have a fireplace, too, for them to keep warm 'cause it could get cold up here on the hill.

B: My house is big enough to cover the whole top of the hill, and it's a long way up here.

A: My house isn't that big . . . you live in yours all the time . . . but Kevin and Diane are just staying here for a while.

A: I think I need some trees by the lake . . . something else [besides stones]

A: Here's twig . . . I got a Good and Plenty box and gum wrapper . . . hey, this [gum wrapper] could be the lake. . . .

B: Yeh! Can I have a piece [of the box] for my sofa and chairs?

A: Here . . . hey, these could be the trees between our property [more stones]

A: Let's change the road and put it here so they can be alone by the lake.

B: OK. Make it deeper down here and curve it over here where your fence is.

A: I'm going to put Kevin in the bedroom 'cause he needs to get his sweater.

B: Mrs. Walton sees Kevin going to the house, and she comes out to talk to Diane.

A: Let's say she already knows Diane 'cause she knew her mother, but she doesn't know that's who it is.

B: OK.

B: Hello, young lady.

A: Oh, hello, Mrs. Walton. I didn't know you lived here.

B: And you're Diane. I didn't know you were coming here.

A: Yes; I just got married and we're on our honeymoon.

B: That's nice.

B: She's going home now 'cause she has supper cooking . . . this is the stove.

A: OK. Kevin is coming back because he saw Diane talking to Mrs. Walton, but he doesn't know who the lady was.

THE SIGNAL FOR THE END OF RECESS. . . .

A: Fooey, we just got it made.

B: You don't even get the time to play . . . somebody will wreck it by tomorrow.

A: Stay here, house . . . come on [dejectedly . . . they walked to the school door slowly, but were laughing and jumping before they went back in the building.]

My youngest son, age 10, setting mounds of soap lather floating around in the bath water. They seemed to be "enemy" objects of some kind, for he soon was observed dropping "bombs" (the washcloth) on them. Sounds of "Bombs away!" alternated with sounds of a diving plane. The plane was his arm and curved hand.

My brother Keith is 7 years old and he would rather play "trucks and cars" than anything.

Keith has in his hand two rocks (one is flat and the other is extremely bumpy). He is in our driveway. He falls to his knees and pushes the gravel away from a spot about four inches by four inches. There he lays his two rocks *very carefully*. Then he "reparks" them. Next he takes the flat rock and "drives" it through the area of gravel, pushing hard and leaving a path behind him. I asked him what he was doing and first he answered smartly "Washing the dog." We both laughed and he showed me his "road grader" which looked a lot like a flat rock. "This is a new substitution and I'm the road maker. This is a pretty good place for new houses 'cause it's close to a expressway." He pointed towards the cement sidewalk and I noticed a yellow chalk line down the middle of the entire walk. We live in a "substitution" (subdivision).

Keith kept making roads for almost an hour, *very carefully*. He made roads that curved, were straight, and finally he got his network of roads to connect to the expressway with *ramps*. This amazed me, even though the ramps were all in one direction—perhaps he meant for people only to get *off* the expressway?

Finally he went back to his first creation where his other rock was parked. During this time he drove his road grader everywhere; he never walked. He parked his road grader and got his other vehicle. I asked him whose car that was and he said it was the mayor's: "Has to inspect my work, lady." He then followed *every* road he had made, slowly. When he reached the "expressway" he turned around and took a shortcut back to the parking lot (through the "un-roaded" area). When he reached the parking lot he pulled up next to his road grader. "Mr. Armstrong, you've done a wonderful job. I'm going to give you a billion million dollars."

'Thanks!" said "Mr." Armstrong. "I'm going to buy a million horses." He *galloped* towards the tree in our yard after he "parked" his "road grader" in the corner of the "lot."

I followed to listen and watch again but he wanted to know why I was tailing him. So I stopped—for a while.

Baby-Sitting for Mike (5):

We went down to the sunny play room in the basement. Mike had a box of snap-together toys: houses, churches, road signs and tiny cars. Mike didn't think he could put them together himself and always got his father to do it; then he'd look at them. This his mother told me. But this time not only did he put them together, but he told me stories about it. Next to us were some empty shelves, which made excellent streets to build houses on.

Mike had a bank, a three story house, a school teacher and banker, church, school, and gas station; included in this collection was a town drunk, and a reckless truck driver. The banker, teacher, and drunk each had a different level of the three story house. The big house on the shelf above was where the grandfather lives. The grandfather made all the students behave in school.

Mike told me a fantastic story about all these people. There was a bar so the drunk got drunk at home and always came sneaking up the back stairs to the third floor by moonlight. (Mike's parents don't drink.) The banker hated the drunk, and was going to the bank because the truck driver was always running into someone and so they needed a new car. The poor school teacher slept most of the time when he wasn't in school. Once or twice the truck driver was hit by the imaginary train, because, Mike told me, the truck driver hit other cars.

When I asked Mike why the drunk had to sneak up to his apartment, Mike replied, "He drank outside by the tree."

Two weeks ago I was at the seashore and I saw some kids building a sand castle.

They built a large castle, in some danger from the waves, with large strong walls around it. It was called "Moo Palace" and was webbed with different passages and rooms. At the top they put a very special shell which they called "the holy grail." Next to it they built the castle of the evil "Beaky-Orc." In front of this castle they built "Beaky-Orc Tenament" which was in "grievous jeopardy from the sea because it had no protective walls."

By and by a wave wiped most of the tenament out, and there were law suits and demonstrations, with "cruel repression" coming from the insidious "Beaky-Orc." "Crazed with gore," Beaky-Orc then marched toward Moo Palace "to capture the holy grail." "A great siege" resulted and "the halls of Moo Palace" were blasted with pom-pom guns.

This incident left quite an impression on me. I went to the sandbox one day with a 2-year-old I was watching. There were three other children already there, one boy about 11 and two girls about 8 and 10. I had seen them before, but I knew nothing about them. They had lots of props to play with, plastic men and women, trucks and a train. I thought they were building a fort. They were busy digging trenches around the fort and also building caves inside the fort. I just sat there in the sand and watched them, inconspicuously of course. Finally, their construction was finished, and they were ready to play. "OK, you put the people on the train," said the boy. The girls put the people on the train. I noticed the boy was talking in a very authoritative voice. The train arrived at the fort. "Unload the people," shouted the boy. "March them to the ovens." OVENS! A cold chill went right up my back. I then realized that the fort was a concentration camp and the caves were ovens. "All right, take them out of the ovens and throw them in the trenches." The girls did as they were told and then covered them up with sand. "We've got to make some crosses," said the girls, and they ran off to look for twigs. The boy busied himself by digging more trenches. The girls came back and laid the twigs in the shape of a cross over the trenches. It seemed the game was now over. They dug up the people and picked up the trucks and the train and left. Before the boy left he kicked at the concentration camp until it again became lumpy sand.

Sobering as this reminder may be, the world needs to remember that child's play explores destruction along with creation, and that the whole width and depth of experience is its realm.

One interesting variant in projected dramatic play is the involvement of living creatures. These two girls (ages 8 and 9) placed their pet miniature turtles inside a cardboard stage set, and instantly invented both plot and dialogue to fit the unpredictable movements of the turtles. This is the script (including an opening familiar to child-lore) written for the announcement of this small scale performance:

> Ladys and gentelmen, hobos and tramps, crosseyed moskitos and boleged ants, Admission is free, so pay at the door, pull up a chair and sit on the floor.
>
> I would like to welcome you all to our show at the turtle Guild theatre tonight. We are proud to present the turtle famile Starring Myrtle turtle as the father, Pogo turtle as the mother, and of course Peppy turtle as the baby.
>
> Now you must use your emagenation because you all no turtles speak a diffrent language that we cannot understand so we and they have decided for somebody else to talk for them but you must pretend that they are talking.

It is interesting to note that the children did not say that turtles cannot speak, but that they speak "a different language": a view being borne out by current studies of whales, dolphins, seagulls, apes. This is another instance of naive perceptions coinciding with the most knowledgeable hypotheses.

A group of third graders played a similar game with the class hamsters (e.g., Mama says to baby, "Be neat! I've told you a hundred times not to eat with your feet in the dish!"). A 4-year-old, playing alone, says, "I'm going to marry this kitty. I'm the mother and the kitty is the daddy, and will go to work." In this case—as with the cat wedding ceremony—the child manipulated the animal as if it were a doll, rather than projecting human thoughts and feelings into its own spontaneous behavior.

Children sometimes dramatically project their images and emotions into unseen presences or imaginary characters, even into the personified parts of their own bodies and minds:

> I often babysit for a little boy named Kurt, who is just 5. He has an imaginary playmate named Ann. She goes everywhere with him, his constant companion. He always talks to her, dances with her, plays with her, etc. Everything he does, she does too. She is very real to him. Once when he was outside playing, he came running into the house crying, "Ann hit me."
>
> . . . Once Kurt was being punished and his mother made him stay in the house. The day after, I went over to babysit and nothing whatsoever was said about Ann. Finally, my curiosity got the best of me and I asked where she was. "In the oven," he replied very cooly. This rather surprised me and I asked why she was in the oven. "Cause she was bad, and bad little girls hafta be punished, just like bad little boys."

Two weeks ago Leslie's mother was in the hospital for ten days. While she was gone Leslie didn't really understand where she was. He told me that, "Little Boy thinks Mother is in the doctor's, but Teddy Bear says she is in jail." It seems that whenever he has conflicting ideas in his mind he lets his "critters" speak for him. Other times he'll say his nose tells him things, or his stomach says no, or his harp says yes. (Harp means heart.)

This little girl (5) was somewhat afraid of the dark. When asked why, she said it was because, "I can hear *footprints* in the dark."

Form, Flow, and Rhythm

"A half an hour is only eight minutes to me," said a 5-year-old. And a moment can also contain an age. In play, as in art and in dream, "linear" time (that which we attempt to measure by clock and calendar to meet utilitarian needs) is less relevant—less actual—than that inner time which has been called the Eternal Now. Tolkien (in reference to the Grimm fairy tale, "The Juniper Tree") writes: "Such stories have now a mythical or total (unanalysable) effect, an effect quite independent of the findings of comparative folklore, and one which it cannot spoil or explain; they open a door on Other Time, and if we pass through, though only for a moment, we stand outside our own time, outside Time itself, maybe." Like myth, fairy tale, and fantasy, child's play can penetrate this unconscious realm and transcend the "minutes" and "years" which have so little meaning for the very young (and the very old?) mind.

Of course, the study of time, of the rhythm and sequence of spontaneous child's play would require volumes, and is still only very partially understood. But these matters comprise so central a part of our concern that some attention must be paid to them here. Two accounts embodying a characteristic flow are chosen as examples:

Episode on a Cottage Sleeping Porch
Characters: Marti (age 6), Carrie (age 5), two baby dolls, assorted clothes.
I was hidden in an adjoining bedroom. I tried to catch all the conversation:

Marti: Pretend I have two babies and give you one.
Carrie O.K.
M: Her bed's up on this pillow. Pretend this time you're the babysitter.
C: O.K.

M: Ding ding (makes the sound of a door bell).

C: If she wets her pants, can I come to her house and change her?

M: If she wets her pants, leave 'em that way. (pause) She was just born pretend.

C: Mine, too.

M: Mine was the youngest, remember?

M: You keep her while I go to a meeting. If she wets her pants, leave 'em that way.

C: No. I can clean 'em. (Sings) Oh la, la, la, la. Up in the shade we go.

M: Ding ding.

C: Come in. Here's your mother, honey (to baby) . Will you take care of my baby while I'm on a trip? Bye, baby. (Kisses baby)

M: Bye mother (imitating baby's voice). You were gone for two and a half hours. You aren't home that quick! Pretend you selled that baby to me.

C: But you give it back.

M: Yeah, when you feel sad. In two days—I'll tell you when. When two days are over. Or maybe eight days. You feel sad. I'll tell you when.

C: (Sings) Oh, sing a song. You see liver, you see chicken, you see liver chicken, you see chicken liver. (Repeats it)

M: Eight days are almost over. Six days, two more days.

C: (Sings) Here's your baby, here's your dime, here's your honey, in the time.

M: It's eight days right now.

C: Hello. How's my baby?

M: Then you sell her to me.

C: Do you want my baby for a while?

M: A whole year.

C: No.

M: Yes.

C: O.K.

M: I'll tell you when the year's over.

C: Can I babysit for you when the year's over?

M: O.K. If I'm going to somewhere.

C: Ha, ha, ha, what a shame of me. (whistles)

M: A year's over.

C: May I babysit for you?

M: No, I'm not going.

C: Pretend, for ten weeks.

M: We're going down to the dock, right? That's a trip for both of us.

C: Thank you for babysitting. It was so helpful.
The players leave for the dock to swim, taking along the dolls.

The control of time is free and instantaneous: going backwards to provide exposition ("Mine was the youngest, remember?"); flying forward ("In two days. . .or maybe eight days. You feel sad. I'll tell you when."); telescoping into the now ("A year's over."). As in adult art, time contracts, crystallizes. The child can go in and out of time, as it were; that is, he can stop the playing at any moment, going outside it, objectively, to direct it ("She was just born, pretend," and "You aren't home that quick !") and coming right back inside the playing, just as rapidly. Discussion and negotiation as to the terms and happenings of the playing can be woven in so that they are not interruptions, but integral parts of the flow. (Sometimes an irreconcilable disagreement breaks down the playing, which then may or may not be resumed again later.)

This account of a somewhat longer playing reveals more of these characteristics of form and flow:

July 4, Four boys playing in two tree forts next to our apartment.
Burke—6 years old
Scott—6 years old
Bryan—4 years old
Max—6 years old

Burke:	Come back. Come back. You went to the hospital.
Scott:	When I went to the hospital they made me blind for one day and 45 minutes.
Bryan:	Ooooooooooh. We're robbers. Cause I don't have none money. kue—kue—kue
Max:	I never get to go and fight.
Burke:	But you're going to get to do something neat in a couple of seconds. Bryan, pretend you got punched.
Bryan:	You can't punch me in the front.
Burke:	Pretend he came from the side.
Bryan:	I'm trying to make you weak—shoo—shoo—That brings you back, right.
Scott:	I'll put you on the operating table.
Max:	You mean I can't come up?
Burke:	No, when you come up, we're at "another" hide out.
Scott:	Let's pretend right now we're at another hide out.
Max:	Let's pretend you take me apart.
Bryan:	Put gas on him to make him forget about everything.
Max:	Okay.
Burke:	Yeah, he did but he didn't make you into a giant man like me—I could destroy him but I won't because he's my master.
Bryan:	How come you got up here?
Burke:	Cause he knows the trap door.

Bryan:	You don't know the trap door.
Scott:	I took out your eye and ear—that makes you unconscious.
Bryan:	Pretend I was walking along.
	Pretend I was walking along.
	Pretend I was walking along.
Burke:	Ow.
Bryan:	That's what I did to you, right?
Max:	Yeah, but I wasn't alive so I didn't go ow.
Burke:	Pretend you taught me how to rob banks.
Bryan:	Pretend I was walking along.
Scott:	Max, you can't come in.
Max:	Pretend that each step I make, I make a hole. Pretend you didn't kill me.
Scott:	Yeah, but I make you unconscious.
Max:	Pretend you knocked the trap door on me.
Scott:	No, Max!
Max:	I'm a whole body.
Burke:	I'm a robot—but you're nothing.
Bryan:	He went up to Mars and came back right through the trap door—and that's you.
Burke:	That's me.
Burke:	You guys stay upstairs. I'm hypnotized so I do what you do.
Scott:	I'm hypnotized too but not so much, so I can do some of what I want. I can eat blueberries.
Bryan:	If you pull the steps all the way down, you die. Pull them only half of the way down.
Scott:	Pretend you said "Go out to the city."
Bryan:	Go out to the city.
Scott:	Start making lazers now.
Bryan:	Max is going to be a cop.
Burke:	But I'm a giant—the strongest one in the game, right?
Bryan:	I'm a little bit weaker. That much.
Burke:	No, that much. That makes it lesser.
Bryan:	I'm from here to the barn weaker.
Scott:	Pretend you said, "Get out and eat mulberries. I like the color of your face."
Bryan:	Get out and eat mulberries. I like the color of your face.
Scott:	You go out and eat coconuts.
Burke:	You ate them with shells on.
Max:	I know.
Scott:	This is a hide out and you can't see it.
Max:	Yes. I have x-ray eyes.
Scott:	Pretend I have a bioctic eye.
Bryan:	Ku—ku—ku—ku

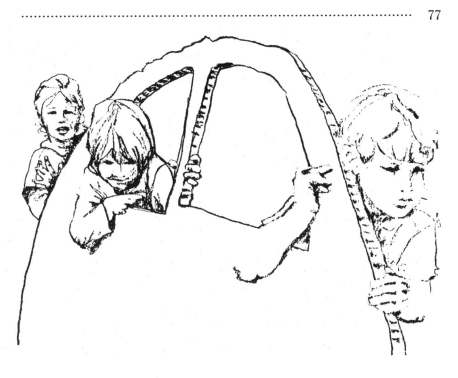

Bryan:	No, a human eye.
Scott:	Pretend I have a fire ball, making smoke.
Burke:	Pretend that Max is dropping from here to the ground.
Scott:	Max is unconscious. I pushed him down.
MAX:	Pretend I have a broken arm.
Scott:	I just put a cast on it.
Burke:	Pretend you say I make the rays more powerful.
Burke:	Max, you're blinded when I go in for a day and 45 minutes.
Scott:	Choo—choo—choo—
Bryan:	Why did you do that?
Scott:	Rob more banks.
Bryan:	Pretend I didn't do it.
Burke:	Pretend all of a sudden I went out of your power.
Bryan:	Scott, the minute you start coming, you're dead because I smashed your raft.
Burke:	Throw him out. It's a dead body.
Bryan:	No, he comes from another planet. Put him in a case. We collect them.
Burke:	I choked him by the chain. See blood come out. Comes out of his mouth.
Scott:	But I'm already dead.

Burke:	I drink the blood. It makes me stronger. It makes me follow your orders.
Scott:	Take out my parts.
Bryan:	No that only works on a robot—so you're still dead.
Bryan:	Max, you come now. You fall through the trap door. We put gas on you so you can't remember this place.
Burke:	Rays are coming out of my belly button. Bryan, you shoot up a ray. This is one that goes up.
Bryan:	Get the money and everything out of the way. We'll chain you up.
Max:	And pretend that I make them think I was a cop and got away.
Scott:	Yeah, but you lost your gun.
Bryan:	Put the gas on so he can't remember.
Burke:	Max, I have to do something for you.
Scott:	Give me the money, Burke.
Burke:	I put the gas on you so you fall down.
Max:	No, I started down.
Burke:	I did it while you were busy.
Scott:	I took your belly button and put this in. No, you can't get free. You don't have any arms. I do. I have an arm and an eye. I'm not bioctic yet. I pressed it all the way down.
Burke:	Now you know what you do.
Max:	I'm a robot now. I do what you say.
Burke:	I will test my strength now.
Max:	I do what you say.
Burke:	You're about to see it.
Scott:	Choo—choo—choo—choo
Burke:	Chain him up.
Scott:	I killed you.
Bryan:	No, Burke, all we have to do is press this down. Max, you're not supposed to do that.
Max:	Real people have eyes open.
Scott:	Yeah, but you're bioctic.
Max:	Yeah, but my eyes are still open.
Bryan:	I made a formula out of this blood.
Max:	I will do what you say.
Scott:	He's alive now.
Burke:	You do what I say, Max.
Scott:	He has to feed me blood every two weeks. Pretend there was a person walking there and I pressed this down.
Bryan:	When do you push the ray and have the trap door come down?

Burke:	I have two laboratories. Let's go to the other laboratory.
Scott:	Don't forget your rays and money.
Bryan:	Say Scott, there's a stick over there—will you get it. Thanks. Hey, Scott, bring the car too.
Burke:	You press this lever down so I'll go out. This is the lever.
Bryan:	You come up to my planet. I lost all my parts. You say, what's going on?
Bryan:	This is the planet I went to.
Burke:	Me too.
Bryan:	No, Burke.
Burke:	I took a space ship.
Scott:	I shoot the ray at the planet, I'm at the planet. Burke, it's only fair if you and me are the same strong.
Burke:	No.
Scott:	Well, in the next chapter I'll be as strong.
Burke:	I only want to play this chapter.
Bryan:	Max doesn't play fair; he has to go up into the sky.
Scott:	It's not fair. You're always stronger.
Burke:	Why do you want to be as strong as me.
Scott:	It's not fair for you to always be stronger.

Observations: It was fascinating the way the boys stayed right in the pretense. Each had a definite role. The leader was the 4-year-old, recognized as such and often making suggestions to the players if they showed signs of boredom. The term "pretend" was often used. They were very congenial the entire time, keeping their concentration on the play itself.

The above sequence may at first seem chaotic, or at least incoherent, but it is also possible that the high, internal form of true dramatic play is present. It is consistent within itself, with a free-associating, dream-like order natural to the young child and to the adult's creative processes, in which uncensored, intuitive, divergent thought is followed freely; and periodically met and shaped by conscious, convergent thought.

Here is an account which exemplifies another aspect of spontaneous play-form: a series of episodes taking place over an extended period (in this case hours, sometimes days or months), each with a separate unity, but connected together by theme, role, or action—like a novel or a scenario:

The day of advance registration was spent on the porch of my boyfriend's fraternity house watching a group of movers, city officials, policemen, telephone company workers, and tree trimmers try to move an octagonal shaped house down Washtenaw. They started in the morning but it was a long job, and by the time the children were returning from school the house was approximately one foot farther down the street than it had been when they left. The only difference now was that most of the trees had been cut down and there were branches lining the streets.

There were many games going on in the branches which lay around, from one group who were playing Davy Crockett at the Alamo, to one boy, who had been convinced by a group of little girls that he was Prince, hacking his way through the thicket to find Sleeping Beauty.

They soon tired of the branches and decided that they would imitate the workers with all their machines. The only problem was deciding who would be foreman. After quite a hassle it seemed to be between two boys, each trying to convince the other that he was best. One boy was much smaller than the other, but the small boy seemed the mightiest. Finally, after finding no other way, the big boy shouted, "I'M foreman and that's that!" The other children inquired as to why he was the leader; when he answered he looked right at the littler boy and said, "Because I don't have any holes in my shirt." The little boy did not seem the least bit bothered by it and got right into the game. The older boy perched himself in the middle of a shrub and started shouting orders to his machines.

Soon the children tired of this game too, and sat down for a while to think up another one. The big boy suggested that they run up on the porch and jump over the trees that grew up the side. So the procession started; run up the porch, jump over the tree, roll down the grass and start again. The boy who could not be leader in the first game didn't participate but sat on the lawn and watched. Finally he got up and walked up on the porch. He started to run and take a leap, but instead of jumping over the bush he landed smack in the middle of it.

We spectators were all afraid that Marvin (by now we had learned his name) had suffered another defeat, until a wide grin spread over his face. He put his arms out to the side and rested them on branches, giving the effect of sitting in a big easy chair. He then hollered "Stop! We are now going to play factory." Everyone stopped at the sound of Marvin's voice calling their attention. He then went on to inform them that they were now the machines since he was sitting in the foreman's chair.

The house started to move a few minutes later so the game broke up, but Marvin came to sit on the steps with us. We told him we were very proud of him being able to be leader after all, and he said, "You guys must have thought I was pretty dumb at first, but I fooled you. I knew I couldn't climb up in that tree and take the seat away from Harry so I had to think of something else. Don't worry about me, I'll get along." With that he brushed off his pants and left.

"So I had to think of something else." Flexibility. Change.

Free and Rapid Change in Play

Another element of play-form, another approach to understanding its process, is its *flexibility* (what Gordon calls plasticity). The freedom to *change* instantly, in response to a fresh stimulus from either within or without, is essential to spontaneous playing. Again it is useful to refer to the mental powers released in dreaming, when the mind reaches a condition of optimal freedom of association. This condition—also characteristic of adult creative thought—is fundamental and natural to child's play. The adult observer who has lost the habit of "winging it"—of letting the mind fly free—finds it difficult to follow; indeed, however keyed in the observer may be, this flow eludes observation. It is easier to do than to watch: involvement drama, rather than spectator's theatre. Any one of us is capable of dreaming more than we can remember or analyze. Nevertheless, the keen student *can* see and hear this valuable flow *if he is willing to believe it* (to suspend judgment), and *if he can accept the fact that it is impossible to understand it all.* Certainly it is necessary to resist the urge to comprehend it at the moment of its happening; what matters is to catch the evidence before it vanishes. This life-study (like all study) is in fact an act of faith, postulated on the basic assumption that meaning is there, waiting to be discovered. "All play means something," asserts Huizinga; it "contains its own course and meaning." Free, mercurial *change* is not a failing, but an essential element of its underlying order:

> Observation of Nursery Group
> The situation begins when Lyle asks Jamie if he wants to play policeman. Jamie agrees, and Lyle assigns to him the role of the robber. Lyle runs over to a bench with a steering wheel attached, jumps on and says, "This is the police car," then makes siren sounds. The siren attracts four of the girls, Chesca, Janice, Lauren, and Angela, who all jump on the car for a ride.

> L: "No, no, this is a police car. No people on the police car," as he unsuccessfully attempts to push them away. Meanwhile, Jamie has left the play and has wandered over to the sand table.

> L: "I'll have to shoot you off. Now I can't go cause you're right
> on my gas tank. Get off."Angela protests that Chesca should
> drive the police car rather than he. Lyle finally clears the
> girls off his car and begins to drive furiously, siren-screech-
> ing loudly. Angela then announces that she is the mommy.
>
> L: "No, no, no, no! We're playing police. You're police
> woman."
>
> A: "No, I'm police *girl*."

Lyle continues driving, but soon gets off the car to approach me. While he's gone Chesca takes over his place on the car and starts to drive. This brings Lyle right back into the play shouting, "I'm the driver. I drive!"

About this time there is a switch in emphasis that completely leaves me. The emphasis of the play switches from police to house. This is first indicated to me by Lyle announcing, "I'll put it into the refrigerator, honey." There is a jockeying of roles with Chesca and Janice arguing as to who will be the mommy. Janice wins and Chesca accepts the role of the little girl and begins to sweep the floor of the house corner, which is bordered on one side by the po-lice car bench. Lyle, in the meantime, has become police father, and begins to work on the lock of the jungle-gym jail.

(Note: An interesting point is how fast the children can find a place for themselves in a quickly-changing situation, and how they can, with a whim, involve a past role into a new role, for example, Lyle's becoming "police father" in the house play. They will repeat, over and over, their new role until the rest of the group accepts it.)

During this exchange, Lauren has moved away from this group and has become a ballerina, dancing in front of the one-way observation mirror. My attention is directed towards her for only an instant, it seems, but when I return to the house corner I find that Lyle is in the process of "busting" his former wife and daugh-ter, Janice and Chesca, both of whom are now robbers. Neither girl is in jail for long, choosing instead to risk the dangers of a break-out! Chesca's escape is successful, but Janice is re-captured by Lyle, who puts her back under lock and key. (Just before the recap-ture, there was an attempt by Lyle to get the girls to commit a rob-bery, but neither would have it, so he started to re-arrest them.)

Chesca's escape culminates in her taking part in a ballet with Angela and Lauren. The latter two girls are ballerinas complete with tutus, and Chesca is the audience, while the record player is the or-chestra. The dance is done to the popular tune, "Colors." The per-formers hop and skip in circles to the music, the climax of the number coming as Angela spreads her legs and Lauren crawls through them. Both girls then fall down, one upon the other, Chesca applauds and laughs, and the group moves on to an entirely new activity.

Observations, questions and notes: Observing 4-year-olds is difficult, because 1. they move and talk very quickly, 2. their play themes change so rapidly, and 3. children can enter and leave a single situation several times in a short span of time. The continuity doesn't seem to break for them, as they are very fluid and mobile in this respect, but it wreaks havoc on the unpracticed adult eye.

Jet Engines—Sparklers on the Fourth of July led to several flights and crashes of jet planes as they were maneuvered back and forth and up and down the back yard. Of course, if you have a jet plane with all that beautiful fire, something must endanger that plane. Therefore, another set of sparklers became machine guns with accompanying noise, leading to eventual extinction of the jet planes. From this idea sprang others. For instance, one child said "Look at me. I'm the moon." Another child became the satellite around the moon. The ideas for movement and objects can vary rapidly. Nothing stayed the same very long.

My husband and I are quite fond of our two neighbor children, Jeffey, who is 4, and Mary Clark, who is 5. They remind us so much of our children, Bill and Mary Ann, twenty years ago. They play in much the same manner as our children did. For example on Friday the following scene took place:
Jeffey and Mary are playing in the general vicinity of one another in their back yard. Except for an occasional glance you would not know they were even aware of one another's presence. Mary is skipping rope. She isn't very good at it for she stumbles badly. Jeffey is running around his fenced back yard. At present he is barking wildly.
Suddenly as if by prearrangement both children change their activities. They leave their back yard and begin playing in their carport. Mary picks up her new Betsy Wetsy and begins feeding her. She is every inch the mother. She feeds it, changes its diaper, fusses over it, scolds it, spanks it, kisses it and lays it down in its bed. Jeffey jumps into his toy automobile that is parked beside his daddy's boat. He drives as rapidly as possible out to the sidewalk. He soon spies a familiar adult, my husband. Jumps out of the car, looks at his rear right tire, shakes his head, turns to my husband and says, "I've got a flat tire, can you help me fix it?" They work very hard taking the wheel off and fixing the imaginary flat tire. After it is fixed Jeffey jumps into his car stating, "It won't go, it's out of gas." He unscrews an imaginary gas cap, inserts an imaginary dip stick into the tank, confirms that he is out of gas, dashes into the house, brings out a glass full of water, brings it out to the car, drinks the water, and drives off with an apparent full tank of gas.

To watch children invent their games is fascinating. In fifteen minutes I saw a group of children (around 6 and 7) change games three times. First the large mound of dirt was their airplane, then it was the lookout tower for forest fires and finally an island in the middle of the ocean.

Second Grade:
I tried to hurry him up before he missed his bus. I said, "Craig you are one of the slowest people I know—hurry up!" He then began to use his umbrella as a cane and started to walk like an old man. He was very realistic, even to his shake and extremely small, slow, unsure steps. From there he became an umbrella-swinging, light stepping dandy. Then he tucked the umbrella under his arm and became a businessman. When he caught up to his friends, he opened and closed the umbrella to shoot all around him. He then opened it (Mary Poppins?) and "flew" the rest of the way to the bus.

Pat, the 9-year-old next door, was delighted with my jewelry case and particularly with my long string of beads. She suddenly became a gypsy with long beads, a dowager with beads wrapped up to her ears, a teen-ager with a bead hairband and a dancer with beads afly.

"The play-mood is *labile* in its very nature," notes Huizinga, "At any moment 'ordinary life' may reassert its rights either by an impact from without, which interrupts the game, or by an offense against the rules, or else from within, by a collapse of the play spirit, a sobering, a disenchantment." Consider this event, for example:

Chuckie and Billy were playing with assorted blocks during free play in their kindergarten class. I went over and asked what they were building and was told rather indignantly, "It's a castle; What do you think it is?" Billy added, "You know, the old kind." Neal came over and asked if he could play and was told that this was only a two-man castle, but he could drive the car around if he wanted to. He "drove" around for a while, then became a battering ram and the castle was quickly demolished.

But characteristically, sudden changes of role, direction, scene, action are woven into the continuity of the playing with remarkable strength and mobility:

Carla (4) had made a house in the middle of the floor. It had a kitchen, a phone, and a bed. I was invited for coffee, and after knocking I was admitted. The walls were moved to give me room to sit down. After coffee was served Carla decided to go shopping while I minded the children. I was given strict instructions to whip them if they were bad, but before I even met the children Pammy and her daughter came to visit.

"Get your kid outta here. She's bleedin,'" said the owner of the house. (Pammy's often-bathed daughter was dripping water through the cracks in her arm joints.) I suggested that Carla phone the Doctor. Carla picked up the receiver and dialed someone better. BATMAN. Luckily we had three Batmen and one Robin hovering about. "Take this baby to the Doctor, she's bleedin'." The first Batman said in his gruff Batman voice, "Hell no!"

(The Batmen were Batmen because they were wearing their hooded winter jackets by the hood and the strings were tied around their chins: the rest of the coat was tied around their shoulders). They wore their Batmasks, a piece of construction paper with two eye holes, tied in the vicinity of their faces. If you didn't make a mask that day you had to be Robin. Batmen had to be terse; the less said, the more like Batman. Darryl, David and Charles were Batmen; Leslie was Robin. I've decided that part of Batman's appeal is that he provides a very masculine figure for little boys who have no male figure in the house to imitate.)

"This baby's run over by a car, and both her arms are fallin' off," pleaded Carla. Pammy was cuddling her baby and telling her that she would be all right. "This is bleedin' over my floor." "OK," said David Batman. Pammy handed her child to David Batman who held her by one leg. "Wait!" yelled Carla, "Gotta find her arms!" After hunting in the "street" she found two arms and gave them to Leslie Robin.

The Batmen spread their capes, and with many sound effects charged to their Batcars. Batmen sped around the room several times and returned to Carla. Pammy had disappeared. Handing the baby to Carla, Darryl Batman said, "It died." Carla threw the doll into the large play house, and came back dressed in heels, gloves, skirt, and—getting a hat—came to say good-bye. She borrowed some money and went shopping.

The mythic phoenix, rising anew from its own ashes into another life, is never "too frequent"; it is a phenomenon which—translated into personal symbols—is not surprising to children at play. Within that sphere, where they draw on very deep levels of being, transformations are commonplace, and Change is an elemental Constant.

CHAPTER SIX

....

Seriousness, Solitude, and Secrecy

"We can begin by saying that all play, both of children and of grown-ups, can be performed in the most perfect seriousness. . . . This intensity of and absorption in play finds no explanation in biological analysis. Yet in this intensity, this absorption . . . lies the very essence, the primordial quality of play."

Huizinga

"The child's best loved and most absorbing occupation is play . . . every child at play . . . creates a world of his own. . . . It would be incorrect to think that he does not take this world seriously; on the contrary, he takes his play very seriously."

Freud

" . . . Absorption is being completely wrapped up in what is being done, or what one is doing, to the exclusion of all other thoughts, including awareness of or desire for an audience. Sincerity is a complete form of honesty . . . bringing with it an intense feeling of reality and experience. . . . "

Peter Slade

The common attitude expressed in our language when someone says, "That's child's play," is that the matter referred to is so simple as to be beneath contempt and that it is not to be "taken seriously." Yet thoughtful attention to play reveals that it is in fact complex beyond our present comprehension, potentially containing all of human achievement and aspiration; and that it is charged with the most profound seriousness. Concentration, simply defined by a 10-year-old boy as "thinking very hard about one thing," is characteristically present in genuine, spontaneous play—intense *"centering"*:

> As I walked down the street, I noticed three children, two boys and a girl, kneeling in a close circle with all their attention focused on whatever was in the middle of them. They didn't notice me so I slowed my pace so that I could notice them. They were nestled together in the crook of an overturned lawn chair and on the other side of the lawn chair was an old wooden horse that looked like an old rocking horse without its rockers. As I passed them I saw the object that was the focus of their attention, a short (no more than eight inches) broken branch from a tree with a piece of string tied to the middle of it. All three of them were working to get this stick into the ground, one of them by turning the stick, one by digging with her hands at the base and the other by pounding the top with some object in his hand that was too small to distinguish. They were mumbling excitedly to one another, but though I was no more than five feet away at the closest point, I could not make any words out—it seemed that quiet under-the-breath talk was essential at this point. Passing them I noticed the younger of the two boys look at me, or I should say, sort of look at me without really seeing me as soon as it was apparent that I was no threat of any sort. I walked slowly on, hoping to catch a glimpse of something else that would cue me in to what they were pretending, but the stick was being very obstinate and they were being very persistent. As I walked back by some ten minutes later, it was apparent that something had disrupted their play. The girl and the younger boy were standing off a way, with the other boy standing by the overturned chair and the horse, saying, "If you want me I'll be in the driveway," in the tone of voice that suggested a disagreement of some nature. The other two children then turned and walked away.
> . . . I noticed most the *spell* that the children had surrounded themselves with—it was so heavy that a person (me) walking by on the street could not break into it; they finally broke it themselves over some disagreement. . . . I can see that what their dead earnestness—their spell—actually means is intense concentration and involvement in what they were doing. . . . There was something about what I saw that made me feel young again and excited about life and all its mysteries. . . . These children were involved in an *action, a struggle in the world they had created for themselves.* They had a stick, a chair, and a broken rocking horse which for them were magical ingredients for their step from this world to that one in their minds: a world that they could all enter together. I just wish that we could all hold onto that power.

The circle, the spell, the struggle, the earnestness: this perceptive student has, in his own direct observation, discerned some of the same psychological states noted by such other students of the human condition as Freud. "Play casts a spell over us;" says Huizinga, "it is 'enchanting,' 'captivating.'" The compelling seriousness of his play literally *holds* a child in this way; play is a necessity which *must* be attended to:

> One day while everyone else was out at recess one of the boys came back into the classroom (second grade) very quietly and slipped into the rocket. I heard him moving around in the rocket and mumbling. I asked what he was doing, taking a trip etc. He said, "No, I had to finish talking to the Martian." I said, "Oh." Then he proceeded to tell me how they had been talking earlier that morning before school, but were interrupted when school started, and he hadn't had a chance to sign off.

> Last evening I baby-sat for Randy (7) and Billy (5). Their parents had just bought a new house and hadn't gotten the upstairs hall rug yet. The only thing that they had protecting the wooden floor was the brown paper that the builders had left. This paper runner wasn't as wide as the hall; there was a space of about three bare inches between the runner and the wall, on both sides. As I was putting the boys to bed they decided that anyone who stepped on the brown paper runner was in quicksand and would be lost forever. We were all originally included in this life and death game; however it soon became obvious that my feet were just too wide to let me play as I was sucked into the pit on my first step. Randy and Billy continued playing this game as they made the necessary trips back and forth from the bedroom to the bathroom. What surprised me the most was their sincere conviction that the runner *was* quicksand. Both boys would clown around in the bedroom and bathroom, but when it came time to walk along the quicksand they were quiet and *deadly serious*. As it turned out, neither boy stepped into the quicksand (they must have played this before and practiced). *I was truly surprised at the gravity with which this game was played.*

There can be no doubt that the seriousness of genuine *play* is akin to that of the artist, the scientist, the brain surgeon at *work*. The *process* demands absorption, and the player/worker *willingly* becomes totally immersed in it.

Solitude

> I found Mary (7) after dark, sitting on a big stump way out in the back yard. I sat beside her. She leaned against me and announced that she had said a poem. I asked her to say it for me—and then over and over again so that I could write it down when we went in. Here it is:

Sometimes it is nice to be *alone*
—and quiet.
Think of all those kids who have no place
to be *alone*
—and quiet.
I wish they could be *alone* here
where it's peaceful
—and quiet.

Children need and seek some times for solitude, for meditation, and for absolutely private inner and outer play. To draw on their own resources, to connect with their surroundings, to weave their own spells—unbroken by any other mind—is requisite to their development. The teacher or parent who is driven always to organize and occupy the child's life—with an overwhelming assault of lessons, clubs, company, television—is unwittingly depriving him of a basic necessity. In retrospect, we see how many of the samplings of play presented earlier have revealed the child playing alone.

These further observations clearly focus on the exploratory freedom and control possible in *solitary* play:

One boy was taking out the garbage and as he set the can down by the curb, I guess something interesting caught his eye. He was, I estimate, about 11 years old, but I can't be sure; he was a pretty big boy, but looked very young. Anyway, he pulled out a broken broomstick—the bristles were pretty sparse, but the broom was cracked in half. He took the broken half in his hand (the bristles facing away from him), and held it as if he were about to fence. He made a Z in the air and began fighting very hard. Then he swung it like a bat a few times. He stood it up, leaning it against the can, and started to talk to it (I couldn't hear because I was too far away). He took some of the bristles in his hand and shook it up and down. He walked away just a few feet, then turned around, threw his arms into the air, looked at the broomstick and really yelled, "I don't know what to do." It didn't last any longer because his mother quickly opened up the door and called him in.

One little girl was playing in the backyard alone next to my parents' house. She is about 8 years old. She had a large piece of cloth draped around her head and she was holding it with one hand under her chin. She was walking around the backyard taking large steps and she looked around to see if there was any cloth trailing behind her. There was a little and she pulled it down so there would be more. She took a stick in her hand and walked around and kind of hit things; she swung at the bushes and hit her swing set. Then she twirled around pointing the stick to the sky. She said, "I rule here," and then began walking and twirling every so often. She sat down and began waving her stick and started talking, and I couldn't figure out what she was saying. I then realized she was making up words of her own. She yelled out, "I am Unda [or something to that effect], I am Unda;" she said it three times, gradually louder each time. She sat down on her swing (making sure the cloth was trailing) and began swinging and waving her stick. She quickly got up, touched her stick to a ball lying next to the swing and then picked it up very carefully and stroked it. She said to the ball (very quietly), "Shh, don't tell anyone you're the royal jewel." She then tore some grass from the ground and put it over the ball as if to bury it. She started to touch things with her stick and then "bury" them in the same manner. She took a leaf, a sand bucket, a rock and some things I couldn't see clearly, and covered them. When she finished she said in a pretty loud voice, "Now don't any of you play when I am gone." She then walked into her house.

To be absolute monarch of all you survey! Power.

Chris, my 3-year-old cousin, said he built a big building with his blocks, but when he thought it was high enough, his "self" said he should put on one more block. "But I said to myself: 'Self, it will fall.' But Self did it, and it fell."

This child vividly reminds us of a sometimes forgotten fact: that *desired solitude* does not mean loneliness; instead, it can be the time for letting out the inner persona—a rich opportunity to be (for blame, for praise, for question, for company . . . for *authority*) "*by* your*self.*"

Secrecy and Privacy

"The exceptional and special position of play," says Huizinga, "is most tellingly illustrated by the fact that it loves to surround itself with an air of secrecy." Whether solitary or with others, true play requires some degree of privacy, even the mystique of secrecy. When we consider that in the process of genuinely playing, the deepest thoughts and feelings are touched and released, the element of *risk* becomes apparent. *Protection* against trespassers in what has even been called the *sacred* play-realm *must* be insured, in the same way that a holy place of worship must maintain sanctuary against violation by non-believers.

Belief is the key, it seems; the outsider "breaks the magic world," as Huizinga puts it; "he robs play of its *illusion*—a pregnant word which means literally 'in-play.'" Evidence of this appears over and over in students' findings:

> While we were walking up to the house, I came across a boy of about 8, hanging by his legs and arms in a tree. He had a rope (clothesline) rigged up in a tree to reach the ground with. He was also dressed in a cape (pillowcase).
> "Who are you?" I said. "Are you Batman?"
> The boy quietly said, "No."
> "Well then, are you Superman?"
> "No," again quietly.
> "Well then, who are you?"
> "I'm just me."
> I later learned that he *was* playing Batman. But I'm afraid that he thought I would laugh at him if he said that. Perhaps he did not think this stupid, inquisitive teen-age girl (he has a sister the same age as I, who belittled him quite a bit even while I was there) could understand his being Batman.

To be laughed *at,* to have one's most precious thoughts mocked, ridiculed, is naturally feared and avoided. Scorn withers—or at least drives underground—imaginative experiment, whereas *trust nurtures* it:

> I was returning from choir when I noticed two small boys playing in the partial stump of an old tree that had been cut down by the city a few days before. When I got up closer I could see that one of the little boys was that same one that I had had the talk with a few days before. I asked them what they were playing. The one little boy replied, "We used to play cowboys and Indians around this tree before it was cut down. I would be the cowboy and Billy here would be the Indian. I would catch him and tie him to the tree and burn him. Now that they cut the tree down we hide our pirate gold in the stump." I asked, "What is the pirate gold?" The two boys whispered to themselves for a minute. The one boy said, "If you promise not to tell anyone what it is I will show you." I promised. They carefully dug up a little marble bag that was filled with bottle caps. I was allowed one fast peek and then the bag was once again buried. I said good-bye and left; the boys went back to their playing.

> I have a cousin, Kathy, who is now in the first grade. For Christmas she received a little dresser with mirror, powder, lip-

stick, rouge, comb and brush. Along with it came a picture of a little boy to set on the dresser. Kathy spends a good deal of her time in front of the dresser and when she leaves the house, she carries the picture in her purse. One day I asked her, "How's your boyfriend?" and she answered in a whisper: "Don't say it in front of people."

Two children, a boy about 9, and a girl about 7 were seated in a spaceship ride in a department store. They were arguing. The boy wanted to go to Jupiter to see if he could capture the monsters that live there. He wanted to bring them back so our scientists could study them. The little girl wanted to go riding around in the spaceship collecting stars. I had been standing at a near-by counter pretending that I was looking at something. As I walked by them the little girl immediately stopped her play and poked the little boy so that he would stop also.

Two sixth grade boys—I was doing some classroom observations; the teacher didn't acknowledge my entrance (I tried to be inconspicuous but that's hard to do). Two boys were very interested in my presence and seemed to be puzzled. I was just within hearing range and caught part of their conversation, "She must be a Russian spy, I just bet ya, look at the way she keeps watching all of us, and she's writing things down too." They had been studying current events and social science and these two were incorporating me into it. I spoke to the teacher afterward and hoped she explained my visit to them.

Kari has just found herself in the floor length mirror we have in the back of our living room. When she thinks that no one is looking she looks in the mirror and talks to the girl on the other side.

I went out and we talked for awhile. I asked him if he ever played "Pretend." He said, "Oh, yes'm, but I never tell anybody what I pretend, 'cept once in a while my dog."

My daughter and I were visiting with a friend one afternoon when she overheard me say, "It's fun to listen to children talk to each other when they play." I guess a child is *always* taking notes on what adults say, because she immediately spoke up and said, "I'll tell you a secret, Mom. Children don't like it when you listen to us. Guess we'll have to send out more spies."

Ironically, the "secret" told here is that child's play itself is secret—except (only "once in a while") from those who can be absolutely trusted not to break faith and talk (like "my dog"!). Believing and making, making believe, are cherished acts—treasures to be guarded from any invader who might undervalue or even destroy them. So the requisite secrecy becomes understandable as a corollary of the fact that Huizinga crystallizes: "The child plays in complete—we can well say, in sacred—earnest."

....

CHAPTER SEVEN

Playing with Grown-Ups

Admission into the Realm of Play

If, wherever treasure is, it must be guarded against theft and destruction, it is also happily true that those who possess it have the power to give it away. It is only necessary to *recognize* and accept the treasure when it is offered. Sharing this wealth seems to be a natural impulse of childhood, and in the beginning children are not only willing but eager to admit "strangers" into their sacred realm of play. The only key is keeping the faith; any true believer is permitted to enter if he proves himself trustworthy. Children do not come into this life with any innate prejudices against anyone; adults inadvertently *earn* children's suspicion by revealing a loss of playfulness:

> A little boy of 3 was playing in the entry hall to the house, which was one step down from the living room. A large ceiling-to-floor mirror faced the living room. The boy sat with his feet in the entry, using the step as a seat. He looked at the reflection in the mirror. He smiled, then frowned, then waved, over and over. He remarked, when asked, that he was fishing and he was waving at the "boy."
>
> Someone rang the doorbell. The child quickly warned the visitor that he was standing in water. The man looked down, then at the boy. Without much enthusiasm he remarked "Oh?" The little boy replied, "Uh huh, but you can't see," and he left the room.

It is simply a question of separating the psychically blind from those who can still see:

As a child, I played house very often. I can remember one experience that thrilled me very much. I had my large baby doll all dressed up with a bonnet on and everything just like a real baby. I was carefully holding her as any proper mother would. An adult was approaching—I felt a pang of selfconsciousness. This, however, quickly disappeared when the *adult truly believed that the doll was a real baby!* Having a great love for babies, I was thrilled that she thought a real baby would be entrusted to my small arms for a walk. I shall always be grateful to the unidentified adult who gave me that pleasure.

A somewhat harder test to pass is seeing that the invisible cannot be seen:

Once while school was in session I was walking down the hall when I met one of the children from the kindergarten class. As we passed he made a horrid face at me. I was somewhat startled and didn't feel such behavior should be allowed. I stopped, turned around toward him and said "Yes?" His eyes became huge with disbelief. "Yes?" I repeated. At this he started to shrink away. He was not afraid, but amazed. "You can't see me, I'm invisible." Not wanting to spoil his play or disillusion him with magic, I answered, "Sorry, my mistake," and walked on. I glanced over my shoulder when I reached the end of the hall. He was standing in the same spot, looking confused—more by my taking his word for it than by declaring himself invisible?

Situation: Persons involved are Matthew, age 4 and myself. Setting: Matt's living room one Thursday evening. Matt is sitting in a very big chair, is in his pajamas and is holding a small white rabbit:

Me: Are you taking your rabbit to bed, Matt?
Matt: Yes, I have to watch him all the time.
Me: Does your rabbit have a name?
Matt: He doesn't have a name because he's been bad.
Me: Bad?
Matt: Yes, he jumps up on the table and takes all the candles.
Me: The candles? How come?
Matt: He needs them to find the carrots at night.
Me: He sounds like a very smart rabbit.
Matt: He is, but he shouldn't get up on the table.
Me: I see.
Matt: Good-night.

"I see." A grown-up still capable of "seeing," in all of its senses—vision, insight, comprehension—is always admissible into the child's world. It is a reasonable enough admission requirement.

Sometimes this adult apprenticeship may take a little time:

Mike And Me: Learning From Each Other
On our first meeting, Mike (7) looked at me and said, "Well, I guess I'll let you tutor me." A few minutes later he said, "Maybe I'll like it." After a couple of weeks, Mike said, "I wish you could tutor me more often." Two months later Mike said, "I want you to be my tutor until third grade . . . (pause) until twelfth grade."

The following excerpted episodes demonstrate Mike's developing trust in his student tutor's collaboration in play:

We were working on addition. We played like I owed him the money. Mike had to add up the totals so that I would know how much to pay him. When he added wrong, I said to him, "Fine, I have less money to pay." Then he corrected the error. He said, "Give me the total." I said, "They add up to zero" (so I would not have to pay him anything). He looked at me, thought for a minute, and then laughed when he realized what I was doing, and added by himself.

I asked him to read arithmetic numbers out loud. Mike pretended that he was a man giving a speech. He held the paper up in front of him and read the numbers off in a very important tone of voice.

We were walking down the street and Mike said, "I'm Batman." I said that I was Robin. It was cold out and Mike stopped and said that he froze to the sidewalk. A little later I said, "What if I froze to the sidewalk?" Mike casually said, "I would pick you up and put you in the furnace."

Mike was eating an ice cream cone. He pretended that he was a grenade devouring the cone.

We were at a restaurant. Mike pretended that he had the coffee and I had hot chocolate. I played along with him. He called the foam in the hot chocolate suds.

Mike had an ice cream cone. He pretended he was Batman and the ice cream cone was Robin. He ate him up—an arm and a leg at a time.

Mike was sitting there. He took a stick and used it as a cigarette. He said that the big sticks were cigars.

He said, "Batman always eats a double ice cream cone—for energy."

After Mike was smoking the sticks, he started barking. I said, "Dogs don't smoke." He said, "This one does!"

For a study break Mike would pretend that he was an airplane. He would run around being an airplane and then come back and tell me what country he flew to.

Mike looked up and saw a piece of paper flying over the lawn. He picked up a pencil and used it as a microphone. He played that he was the man who announces when an airplane is taking off.

We were walking along and Mike said, "I'm a soldier coming back from the war wounded." He then acted it.

Mike said, "Save the popsicle stick. You can sharpen it. In case a robber comes I can stick him with it."

It was raining and we were outside. Mike said, "See, I'm taking a shower." Then he jumped into a puddle and said, "Now I'm taking a bath."

Mike picked up the umbrella, closed it, and used it as a gun. Then he opened it, sat under it and said, "This is my mushroom."

Mike's tutor earned and maintained membership in his inner life because she opened to his playful mind.

> I babysat for two small boys aged 5 and 9 who were intensely involved in a trucking game when I arrived. Around dinner time they did not want to stop to eat. The oldest then announced to his assistant (the 5-year-old) that it was time to pull over to the next stop for dinner. They would then have to drive all night to Chicago. When they were seated they proceeded to order their dinner as if they were in a diner. I took their orders and served them just like a waitress. When they had finished they paid their bill and departed on their journey into the night.

"They also serve who only stand and wait." Grown-ups invited into children's play need to "know their place."

> A little neighbor girl, Cissy, just turned 4. Her mother gave her an old negligee of blue, filmy material. For several days she went strutting around her back yard with her friends. One day, three of them came to my door. Finally, after their hellos, the little boy said to me, "The queen would like to see you, and we are here to take you with us." And there stood Cissy in her negligee at the end of the walk, waiting.

It is the wise person who promptly keeps the appointment when granted an audience by the queen.

> Lenny (5): "Auntie Kay, will you play Doctor with us?" Lenny was the nurse, and Ernie (4) the doctor, and I the patient. As I walked up to the doctor's office (our den), Lenny asked me if I had an appointment? As I began to say "Yes" she blurted out, "No, you don't, but we will squeeze you in." When I was taken into the room I had to lie on the couch. Ernie noticed right away that I had a broken leg and arm, and a very high fever. Lenny was constantly coming over, taking my temperature, giving me shots for the pain, and pushing M&M's in my mouth for the fever. After taking X-rays with my empty camera, Ernie told me that I was lucky not to've gotten killed from the car accident. Now the two of them bandaged my wounds with paper toweling, Kleenex, and tape. It was a long process and when it was completed I felt I couldn't move. I lay there stiff, as two of their friends came to the door. Lenny went to the door, returned and asked for a private conference with the doctor. They both left the room and returned around five minutes later with their coats on, "You can go home now because it has been two weeks since you've been here and you are now better. We have to leave now, so pay us the thousand dollars you owe us!" Luckily I

had enough cookies to pay off my hospital debt and Lenny and Ernie went outside to play.

A treatment not for buying and selling. "Play," says Huizinga, "is an activity connected with no material interest, and no profit can be gained by it."

> Janette (4) and I sat on my bed. We were surrounded by nearly a dozen picture books, half of which we had already studied. Suddenly, Janette spoke up, "This is a boat, okay, Carol?" and she began to rock back and forth. I quickly agreed; thinking this would be a good break from reading all the books Janette kept handing me as soon as I closed the cover on the last one. I gathered up all of the books, and rose from the bed to put them on the nightstand. Janette screeched, "You're in the water! You're in the water!" and bounced up and down with glee. I jumped back on the bed and we continued our cruise. Janette took off her right sock and hung her leg over the side of the bed. She jerked it back again almost immediately and put her sock back on. "It's *cold*," she confessed. During the course of our cruise, we fished (Janette caught Charlie, the Starkist Tuna—Oh . . . the influence of television), drank milk from coconuts and ate fish tails, swam, and took turns sleeping and guarding for "sarks." At dusk, we sailed into port, anchored, and bounced off to Auntie Joyce's for dinner . . . for "sailors get very hungry."

Body and soul; both are understood equally and embraced in the wisdom of childhood.

> Scottie is 5 years old. He has carrot red hair, big brown eyes, freckles—hardly the Al Capone type. As the "grown-ups" sat around the dinner table expounding their after-dinner-chatter, the kitchen door swung open and standing there in all his glory was Scottie, in his father's hat, and machine gun in hand. He was poised in the stance runners assume at the starting line. He swung his machine gun from left to right as he growled, "Don't make a move. Do you hear me? Nobody move." He turned on his 7-year-old sister. "You moved; I saw you." He approached Grandpa, who was sitting at the table. "Mister, gimme all the money ya gots . . . or I'll shoot." Grandpa looked worried as he gave him an empty handful of money from his pocket. "Thank you very much," replied Scottie. He held the family at gunpoint as he made his way around the table. He stopped beside Grandma. "Lady, is this house yours?" Grandma said that it was. "Can I have it?" Grandma looked doubtful, but remained silent. "Can I have it, Lady?" Grandma remarked that it was her house and she wouldn't have any place to live. "Please! You can

live with my Mommy and Daddy . . . Can't she Daddy?" With that, Grandma smiled and told Scottie that since she couldn't just give her only house—how about an extra big piece of homemade apple pie! Scottie yelled, "Oh, Boy!" threw down his machine gun, and followed Grandma out to the kitchen. No sooner had he left the room than he was back again. He skipped over to Grandpa and gave him his "money" back. With a big grin he said, "Here, Grandpa. I'm gonna have apple pie instead." And he disappeared into the kitchen once more.

A robber gentleman honors his debts. The Other world and this one intersect. There is a time for pie-in-the-sky, and a time for pie in the belly.

"Send in the clowns! There ought to be clowns. . . . Well, maybe they're here," says the Sondheim song. A child can share zestful delight in the comedy of the human condition, with an adult capable of laughing without programming:

> There's a kid down the street with whom I often play verbal games. I don't know his name, but he knows mine, and he gets great pleasure out of finding new nicknames for me, such as Ragmop, Ragamuffin, Rags-Scags, etc. One day, while I was mowing the lawn, the boy came pedaling down the street on his Stingray bicycle, yelling his several different nicknames at me at every possible range of his voice. I stopped mowing, leaned against the mower, and prepared myself. "What d'ya say, Rags, Scags, Mags, Bags," were his opening remarks to me. I replied that I was exhausted and that since he was such a charming young man he would probably be glad to mow my lawn for me. Then it happened—before I knew what he was doing he had completely transformed himself from a little boy into a grandmother. He did it with a red sweatshirt that had been wrapped around the handlebars; he took the sweatshirt, threw it over his head, and clasped it under his chin with one hand, while with his other hand he positioned the sleeves of the sweatshirt to fall over his shoulders like a shawl. When he was satisfied with the sweatshirt he reached into his shirt pocket and pulled out a pair of lensless white sunglasses and put them on upside-down. This all took place as he was riding his bike in relatively small circles in front of me, sometimes using one hand to steer, sometimes none.
>
> While he was costuming himself he gradually began talking like an old person. He stuck out his lower jaw as far as it would go and sucked in his upper lip. He then began shaking his head and arms slightly, all the while his voice getting more harsh. He (she) was talking about his (her) nice young grandson who would just love to mow the lawn for me if he were here. Unfortunately, he

(she) went on, his (her) grandson had gone visiting relatives far away and he just wouldn't be able to make it. The grandmother began shaking more violently now, so she had to excuse herself and go home to take her pills. He (she) thanked me for our lovely chat and that little old grandmother rode her Stingray bike down the street—still shaking visibly.

Children can play whole unplotted plots through, with a sensitive grown-up:

> Janette is a petite, honey-haired, blue-eyed 4-year-old. As she entered the room I noticed an excitement about her. She scuttled over to me, grabbed my left arm with both hands, and pulled me from my chair with all the might her body could muster. "C'mon, Carol! I'm the monster and I'm gonna lock you up in my palace!" she proclaimed. She came after me with her arms and fingers stunted in stiff, claw-like fashion. She bared her clenched teeth to me as she made guttural sounds. She proceeded to capture me by stretching her arms as far around me as they could reach. With her cheek pressed against my side, she shuffled me off to an armchair in the living room which served as a prison. She sat me down and reached into her imaginary pocket. She made a snapping noise with her tongue against the roof of her mouth as she turned the "key."
>
> "Help! Help! Where am I? Save me!" I cried. For a moment Jannie looked at me as though her sad blue eyes were going to melt. Then she said (in a comforting tone and much like a Shakespearean aside): "Pretty soon the good monster will come and save you . . . okay?" Without waiting for my reply, she turned and ran to the other side of the room, stopped suddenly, took one last look at her victim across the room, and changed roles. She poised herself in crawling position and started in my direction, assuming her new identity. "Here I come! Here I come to save you, Princess!" Upon reaching my feet, she lifted her torso. "I am the friendly turtle and I came to save the beautiful princess out of the dungeon." With that, she reached for her "key" and unlocked the latch. She pulled me from the chair with both arms outstretched. Her eyes beamed and a glorious smile blossomed from her face as I extended my thanks and praises for my rescue. She took my hand in hers, stood on tiptoe, and stretched up to me so that her breath brushed my hair and tickled my ear as she whispered, "You can go now."

Recognition of the beginning, consent to the ending. "Play begins," says Huizinga, "and then at a certain moment it is over."

> Walking to class, I encountered three little girls, ages 3–5, standing on the sidewalk blocking traffic. As I came up they asked

me to stop and see that this was a toll gate I had to go through. I asked how I was to get through and they answered, "5¢ will open the gates," I replied I didn't have the money, so they got into a huddle and told me to wait until they talked it over. After a few glances and giggling whispers, they came to the conclusion that 2¢ would be sufficient. I said fine and pretended to put the money in one of the little girls' hands. She accepted and was overjoyed with her newly-acquired wealth. The gate opened and I went through, thanking them kindly, and was told there would be no charge for a "nice lady like me" on my return trip through their country.

Coming back through this country I was greeted with open arms and had an escort to the next corner, along with a hundred questions. I felt great—like a queen. I had played the game and they were overjoyed.

The grace to request admission into the magic kingdom brings the joining, the safe conduct, the crowning, and joy.

> May 12,1972 7:30 p.m.
> *Me*: "Would you like to do a story?"
> *Rob*: "Let's do Thunder and Rain!"
> He begins with soft, slow gentle bowing back and forth on the violin strings. I join in on the piano using any group of high pitched notes, playing them slowly over and over.
> *Me*: "The raindrops are just beginning."
> We both accelerate in speed and increase in loudness.
> *Rob*: "Make the Thunder!"
> I run my fists up and down the low pitches of the piano, and Rob, with great excitement, plays fast bows on the lowest violin string.
> *Rob*: "Now make lightning!"

Using my forearm on high pitches I make the crack of lightning. Rob plays squeaky sounds on the "wrong" side of the violin bridge. Then the storm subsides and the raindrops slow down and die away. Together we make slower and softer sounds.

A mother and child in harmony: players playing.

The other day I saw a 2-year-old boy sitting on his mother's lap as she talked for an hour or so with some other people. The child kept himself occupied by exploring what sort of person I was; and more importantly telling me about himself. He began by burrowing his head under his mother's arm, and peeking out again, checking if I was still with it. And I was; so we sat beaming at each other for a while. Then we played the game again. "I'm not here; I am!" I don't know whether children are taught that game or whether it does in fact arise spontaneously. It certainly must be a fundamental human experience; the tiniest child can be absorbed in it for hours. But this game in fact was only the first of many ways of communication: making faces—to be mirrored?—sitting, standing, hanging on Mother's lap in as many different ways as possible, and finally, pulling on mother's hand as though, this time, really to let go. Which in fact he did. All the things the child did had the character of games. The games seemed to have all the progression of discovering; I can exist, I can communicate, I can be alone—or I think I can. But all of these games, if not dependent on, at least are ten times enriched by response from other people.

Indeed the child seeks and needs the mature mind's response and stimulus. The adult who is still able to enter into the child's play *sanctions* and *completes* it; by playing himself, he *validates* and *strengthens* all of the powers thereby naturally exercised. It is adults who can provide the environment which stimulates and allows the child's full development. Albert Rosenfeld, in the *Saturday Review* (August 7, 1976), reports on the experiments of Dr. David Krech, of the University of California at Berkeley:

> . . . "All of the advantages of inheriting a good brain can be lost if you don't have the right psychological environment in which to develop it." Krech and his associates did a now classic series of experiments, raising baby rats in "nursery schools" full of things to keep them interested, amused, and challenged. Rats thus raised not only had a measurably greater *number* of neurons than other rats, but their brain cells were richer in their biochemical content . . . in a stimulating environment, the neurons that already exist can grow larger by some 15 per cent and form myriad new connections. . . . The same appears to be true for humans, Dr. Myron Winick, of Columbia University's Institute of Human Nutrition, has decided after a careful study of starved Korean orphans adopted by American parents. In a new, loving environment, they improved beyond what had previously been thought possible.

The child, in order to realize his potential—whatever that may individually be—requires reassurance from the adult world which he craves to grow into: reassurance that it is natural and useful for human beings to question, to imagine, to wish, to dream, to create.

At the same time—as in all healthy relationships—the adult who can still share in child's play receives at least as much power as he gives. Natalia Satz (founder of the Central Children's Theatre of Moscow) is quoted in her recollections of the Moscow Art Theatre. "Among the actors . . . children and childhood were highly regarded," she recalls, citing their belief that "children should grow up alongside their elders who would then sense each step of their growth. . . it is only when an artist lives with children that he does not lose his quality of creative immediacy. . . . Stanislavski wrote: 'An artist remains to the end of his days a great child, but should he lose the immediacy of a child's point of view of life—he ceases to be an artist.'"

So with just enough sense to hold on to the sacred inheritance to which all are born, growing up need never mean growing poor.

There can always be a 4-year-old queen (sending her servants to your door to say she wants to see you), waiting in her royal negligee at the end of your walk. There can always be tender-loving-care, Kleenex-bound fractures, and miracle medications for a mere airy grand on eternal credit. There can always suddenly be a friendly turtle ("Here I come to save you, Princess!") unlocking your dungeon to rescue you. The gate will always open, and there will never be a toll charge for any wanderer returning to that magic country.

CHAPTER EIGHT

The Play of Words

> When we were children we could have learned so much about children! . . . Now I will never be able to talk with them as I could when I was a child. . . . You can't disguise yourself as a child and mingle in with them or go back to being a child. . . . You *can* try to win their confidence and get them to talk; they want to if you will give them a chance and treat them right.

The 20-year-old man who wrote those wistful words reflected a common feeling. Confronted with the idea that child's play is essential to understand and recapture, the adult may at first feel as if he is trying to decode an ancient, lost language. But aroused curiosity and willingness to make the attempt are usually the key that unlocks the secret. The modern scholar-detectives who first saw the otherwise-hidden Stonehenge inscriptions suddenly revealed by the exactly right angle of sunlight must have felt this marvel: it was there all along, just waiting to be seen. Of course the inscriptions, once seen, have yet to be completely unriddled—still, discovering that they are there, is a beginning.

The constant play of images, ideas, and words which characterizes the child's *talk* is a medium and a message in itself. The secret of being admitted into these marvelous conversations seem "childishly" simple: too simple for most of us who have reached our full height. The secret is to take the trouble to *listen* (a vanishing art in the twentieth-century world). To listen with the whole attention and full intelligence is, of course, not always easy. Prejudice is deep and subtle. Children often recognize society's "double standard" snobbery toward the young, though they may tolerantly marvel at the basis of adult claims to superiority. Once my 7-year-old daughter wrote on a restaurant's suggestion card, in the space after "Rest Room": "Toilet too cold." Her 8-year-old sister said, "Oh, Howard Johnson will know it's written by a child and won't pay any attention . . . but maybe if you write all rough and pushed together so it's hard to read, they'll think it's a grown-up's writing." And there's the story of the first grader who was still seeking reasonable explanations for the puzzling condescension of his reading book's style when he read, " 'Oh, oh, oh,' said Dick, 'Oh, oh, oh.' " (Pause.) "Boy, they sure do talk funny. Maybe he doesn't know too many words." Fortunately, there are a lot of first grades by now stocked with richer reading books, but children cannot always count on the adult world to respect them. In her *Children Go To The Theatre* (translated by Elizabeth Reynolds Hapgood), Natalia Satz recalls being "treated as a grown-up" in her childhood. Referring to the famed Russian theatre artist, Vaktangov, she says that he "had a very special way of talking with children; his words inspired confidence . . . what he said enhanced human dignity, recognizing that even a little person . . . can harbor great thoughts and have creative impulses." She adds further that "we not only had the right but we also had the *duty* to have an opinion."

This important idea brings us to the realization of one of the most insidious hidden perils of prejudice: the unconscious condescension which takes the form of indulgence, permissiveness. It is as insulting and damaging to treat a child obsequiously—to allow license, to make no reasonable demands—as to ignore him. For instance, if an adult is curious about a child's thoughts, it is natural to ask questions:

> I noticed a 4-year-old boy eating the heads—only the heads —off some sugar-cookie horses. He was serious, not saying anything, but deliberately biting the head off—eating it—putting the "headless" body down—and picking up another cookie to repeat the act.
>
> Finally I asked him what he was doing. He looked up and answered, "I'm a giant and I'm biting the heads off horses."

Once her healthy curiosity overcame initial self-consciousness, this student had the good sense to ask a question, and got the fair reward of a straight answer. Now she has *evidence* of that child's dramatic imagining of superhuman power and of the intellectual abstraction involved in hypothesizing a projected relative scale of sizes. And he in turn, has evidence of adult interest in his thoughts. Both are richer for this simple exchange.

Being really honest in human relations involves taking certain *risks,* and therefore requires the courage of conviction. One student, after we had been considering this matter in class, reported this beautiful breakthrough in her second-grade practice teaching:

> *Child:* Our horses were acting funny yesterday. One kept
> jumping onto the back of the other one.
> *Me:* (Silence.)
> *Child:* (Repeats the above statement.)
> *Me:* Guess they wanted to mate.
> *Child:* Yes! I was wondering if you knew!

To meet a child's testing of your honesty is to pass into true communion. It is even necessary and possible for an adult sometimes to admit to the human frailties that children are all too familiar with in themselves:

> A few weeks ago I went to the dentist. My son (8 years old) accompanied me and waited with me in the reception room. We had a short wait before I was called. We browsed through the magazines in the office and chatted quietly.
> Suddenly my son asked: "Mom, do you feel scared about getting your tooth filled?"
> I asked why he questioned this. He pointed out that as I was sitting there with one leg crossed over the other, I was swinging the free leg, and swinging it rather vigorously!
> I admitted only that I felt "nervous" because I didn't *enjoy* having a tooth filled.
> He looked straight at me. "But, you aren't *scared?*" he asked again.
> Looking at that perceptive child, I could not lie. "Well, deep down inside I think I do feel a little scared."
> His smile was totally sympathetic. He then admitted: "I usually am scared, too. I guess nearly everybody would be."
> I replied: "I guess so."
> When I was called a few minutes later my son spoke up: "I'll be right here waiting for you when you're done." His tone was quite protective.

To *face* fear and join in the supportive refusal to yield to it—*that* is courage. But truth has to be practiced, relearned, over and over:

> My little cousin Mike loves cars and anytime he can get you to take him for a ride you are queen. One day he kept begging and begging, "Just around the block." Well, I teased him by saying my gas tank was empty and we wouldn't get very far because we would run out of gas. He looked very sad and said he would get his coat and go outside while I drank my coffee. That lasted about five minutes, when he stopped in saying, "I just was walking by your car and I stopped, so I thought I would see if everything was in working order and the magic windows were up tight in case of rain. I also checked the gas, and it's on *E*; that means empty doesn't it?" I answered "Yes"

with as straight a face as possible and he calmly left the room "to play cars in my bedroom," he said. A few minutes later we heard noises so we went to check. Here he was, shaking his bank "to make money to drive around the block just once." He showed me the pennies and told me he'd "taken care of the gas problem" so I could get my coat and start the engine. What could I say to that? I followed his directions and now have resolved never to lie to a child.

I had a conversation with a 5-year-old girl in the restaurant last weekend. She asked me where my father worked. I told her at Ford Motor Company. Her father said something about Henry Ford which led her to ask, "Is Henry Ford your father?" I said flippantly, "No, but wouldn't it be nice." She looked up at me and said, "Don't you love your father?" After I had reassured her that I certainly did love my father, I vowed to try never again to say anything to a child that might be misconstrued.

Sarcasm is one way to misunderstanding; mealy-mouthing is another:

Setting:	Mama getting ready to go out. Amina (3½) calling up the stairs.
Amina:	"Can I go, Mama?"
Mama:	"I don't think so."
Amina:	"I can go."
Mama:	"No, you can't."
Amina:	"Does 'I don't think so' tells me 'no'?"

On a morning shortly following the Cassius Clay fight, Herbie came into the room (3rd grade) bouncing around like a boxing champ, fighting with someone that I couldn't see and saying, "Look, look Teacher, I'm Cassius Clay."

Me:	Do you like Cassius, Herbie?
Herbie:	Well, I guess *so,* Teacher. He's colored.
Me:	Oh, Herbie, we don't just pick our friends because of their color. We pick our friends because we really like them.
Herbie:	Maybe you pick your friends that way, but you's a teacher.

A moral lecture stops conversation, and this teacher was honest enough in retrospect to catch herself in that dead end.

Sometimes, of course, love is the motive for avoiding open communication, but even then it is a tangled web we weave when first we practice to deceive:

> Mike (10) and Kathy (9) sent me an invitation to their Christmas party at home. K. came running down the stairs acting all excited about Santa's coming; she kept on mentioning Santa. Mike had been told that Santa was his father, and he had promised to keep his sister in the dark, to play along so that she could believe a little longer. . . . Later, after the presents were opened, K. told me privately, "You know something: there's no Santa—Daddy's Santa—but don't tell Mike—I don't want to ruin it for him. You know—I don't think there's an Easter Bunny either, but I'm not saying anything to Daddy because he likes to hide the baskets—and it's fun, too."

Judging by my evidence, this country is full of people innocently keeping this same secret from each other, for fear that someone they love is too young or too old to survive disillusion. My own bittersweet memory of that transition from literal to symbolic is of the same decision: to spare my parents a shock that I feared they might not be ready for. But I was deeply touched by their hopeful, trusting attempt to act out a fairy-tale for me, and moved by the idea of mortals mythically, anonymously bestowing gifts with no thought of being thanked. Maybe these transmigrated legends of reindeer and rabbits are almost the only dramatic play remaining to some adults; it is not surprising that confusion abounds as to the relation between the symbolic and the literal, between child and grown-up. People who are out of practice in believing and imagining are vulnerable to getting wedged between the different planes of reality. Sometimes they have trouble distinguishing between a "lie" and a "story," for instance, like the kindergarten teacher cross-examining a boy who calmly claimed to have crossed the ocean twice that morning already.

In truth, the problem that we so often face in discussions with children is that they ask questions to which we ourselves *do not know but feel we ought to know the answers:*

> Our next door neighbor's 9-year-old son made his first communion last Saturday. He came over to play with our dog and told me about his feelings on the day. He was very upset.
> "I don't think I want to get my communion. I don't want to stick my tongue out at the priest," he stated, folding his arms and shaking his head sharply. He stood in this matter-of-fact state and waited for my reaction. I tried to explain that he wasn't being disrespectful, but helpful, so the priest could give him the host. As I think of it now, I realize that he was still puzzled, and I should have gone further. Further where I do not know!

We were sitting on the front porch of her house, and Elizabeth (2½) was just gazing at the sky for a long period of time. Finally, she turned to me and said, "Auntie Mo, are the clouds swimming in the water?" How does one explain something of this nature to a small child?

"Further where I do not know!" and "How does one explain...?" These words reveal a dawning awakening to the essential fact that a child is asking the penetrating questions about the universe and life that humankind never outgrows. The adult who truly *listens* to a child's questions, and *joins* in the questioning, is inevitably pressed to think more deeply and clearly along with the child. Stagnation results only from "leveling down"; there is danger in the dominance of this kind of non-question:

I mentioned that we were going to have a review—"did anyone know what a review was"—Stevie (6) moans and says in a low voice, "Oh, no." He raised his hand and I asked him if he wanted to tell us what it is. "It's when you go back and do it *all over again.*"

To be admitted into the child's play and into his play of thoughts and words, requires the grasping of one of those basic truths that seem so obvious, once understood. A conversation in the car clarified this for me:

P (7): You know that one, "It is more blessed to give than receive?"

M: Yes?

P: I've been thinking; it must be just as *blessed* to receive.

M: How do you mean?

P: Well, if you want to let the *other* person be more blessed, you have to sometimes be the one that lets *them* give something to *you*. It's not right for anybody to want to be the one more blessed. So you have to learn how to receive. Otherwise they can't give. So receiving is blessed too. Sometimes give, sometimes give *receiving.*

M: I never really thought that through. You're right.

That exchange threw considerable light on the Santa Claus phenomenon, too—for me, at least. As rudimentary a fact of human relations as that may be, not everyone seems to know it:

Susie and Paul came into the drugstore to buy a birthday present for their mother. Susie was 8 years old and Paul was 4. (I know because I asked them and they told me.) Susie and Paul's mother has pierced ears so they had decided between the two of them to buy her a pair of pierced earrings. They each had a dollar but Susie was taking care of all the money. Since it was a weekday and we had few other customers in the store, I was happily able to devote my entire attention to Susie and Paul. I showed them all the two-dollar pierced earrings, taking the racks down from the high cabinet on which they were displayed. The children carefully inspected each pair. Susie favoring the bright flowers and Paul voting for shiny fishes or hanging turtles. Finally the little green fishes were chosen and I wrapped them the best way I knew how, made a special bow for the package, paid the 8¢ tax myself and mistily sent them home, glowing with pride. Half an hour later I looked up to see Susie and Paul and their mother, looking again at earrings—or rather the mother, with unwrapped package in hand, was looking at earrings, for I had returned the racks to their place on the high glass cabinet and the children couldn't see them. I snuck over to Paul and whispered "Didn't she like the earrings?" His glow was all gone and he just grunted a dejected "Nope." I asked the mother, with all the politeness my acting ability enabled me to display, what was wrong with the earrings. She said she had nothing green to wear them with, and then in a confidential aside, as if *I* would understand, informed me the fishes just weren't her style anyhow— they were all right for kids, but————.

This mother's inability to accept her children's present divides her from them, symbolizes a broken connection that will make playing together tonight, talking together tomorrow less likely and less easy. Estrangement happens in such seemingly small ways—in drug-stores, bartering away the little green fishes: unrecognized gifts of love. A loss of blessed receiving.

By contrast, being open to receive a child's gifts (whether in the form of a bouquet of weeds or words) creates closeness. Note this problem-identification-and-solution process, effected with a modicum of sympathy and moral support:

Ellen, a vivacious 6-year-old in pigtails, was always playing grown-up. She imitated most everything I did, from the words I used to the way I dressed. Her favorite person was the same as mine; my boyfriend, Dave. Ellen followed Dave with big staring eyes, and was always quick to hop up on his knee or cuddle up beside him. She came to me one day with a very perplexed look and said, "Lynne, what are we going to do? I love Dave too, and he can only love one of us." I wasn't quite sure what to answer her, until she inquired quite shyly, "Maybe he could love us both?" I assured her he could and her expression softened and she said, "That's good, because I sure do like being in love with a big boy."

A few days later Ellen was back for a girl-to-girl talk. Very solemnly she told me that she had told Dave that it was over. When I asked her reason she replied, "Well, I decided that he was only fascinated with me, ["fascinated" happened to be my favorite word at the time] and he really liked you best. Besides boys my size are more fun."

An experience at 6 to strengthen the powers of decision needed at 16 and 36.

At its fullest, the free, relaxed give-and-take of word-play between child and adult can yield genuine communion:

> Later, my husband, Sally, and I went for a boat ride. The sky was pink in the north, purple in the east, and blue in the west with great globs and shreds of quiet clouds.
>
> Sally rode in silence and then the questions started. "What's the matter over there?" she asked pointing westward. "The sky is gone! What's that black thing?" She meant the shape of the clouds. We decided that it looked like a big bird.
>
> About one more turn around the lake found the stars popping out, and night all around. Sally looked for the big bird and found that it had gone. "Where's the bird?" she inquired as she scanned the heavens.
>
> I said quietly, "What do you think?"
>
> She snuggled deeper in my lap. "I guess he went to bed with the sky," she answered sleepily.

> Michael came home from school one day and said that numbers were the most important thing in the world—I asked why. "Well," Michael said, "there is nothing that you cannot make numbers with. Go ahead and name anything you want and I can make a number go with it." Well, I proceeded to name things like houses and trees, and he found a way to apply a number to anything I named.
>
> A couple of days later, driving in the car, I said, "I've got one for ya, Mike," and I said, *"love*—that is something I'll bet you can't make numbers go to." And he thought for about one second and started bouncing up and down in his seat saying, "Oh yes I can—*it takes two and it makes one!"*
>
> I cherish that moment that Michael and I had as one of our most precious.
>
> He gave me a lot.

It never ceases to amaze me how children perceive and know so many things almost naturally that adults are no longer certain of.

··

CHAPTER NINE

Rememberings:
The Heritage of Play

To open to a child, to say "yes" to the invitation—which is sometimes direct, sometimes covert—to re-enter the magic realm of play: that is one way to regain whatever powers may have been lost in the attrition of aging. Another natural way to recapture the play-spirit is through memory. The adult who keeps always in touch with the child within, who uses and truly takes possession of all that he already owns, knows the best of both worlds. And these two ways integrate, make a circle, unite; the acceptance in the now of children present stirs and freshens the memories, restoring the intuitive powers of childhood; and in turn the summoned memories renew wonder, so that joining in children's thoughts becomes constantly easier and more spontaneous.

The rememberings of childhood, whether by 75, 47, or 19-year-olds—flow from deep wellsprings:

> Looking back to my childhood, I recall another one of my favorite pastimes when I was approximately 7 or 8 years old. In my room, the closet door and outside door were very close together; in fact, the two doors could be pulled together and made a lovely elevator. I used to play department store with my cousin; she would get in between the doors, and I would say "going up" and ask what floor she wanted. She would get off on the floor, and I was then the sales lady for the gift or clothes department. The elevator would then return when a purchase or two had been made and go down a floor at a time, indicating what each floor had on it.

> I can remember playing school very often. I would take very good care of my books and supplies. I was the teacher and one of my friends was the pupil. We had all the furniture arranged as a

classroom. I had all our old schoolbooks and supplies well organized. I had lesson plans made out and taught on the blackboard. We really did do schoolwork. I can remember thinking that I must really try to *teach* my pupils. I took this very seriously. When we ended our play, I had a feeling of accomplishment.

I suppose that this play substantially helped shape my life because I plan on being a teacher. I "played" at what is to be my life's "work."

Another of my favorite pastimes when I was 8 to 10 years old was playing teacher. I would sit at the desk and call the roll, imitating the current teacher. I especially enjoyed writing the notes to excuse the students for being absent. The blackboard was handy and contained the current assignment, since my mother bought the books that I used; I missed school a great deal due to colds. Another favorite area was pretending discipline. I would pick on the "trouble makers" in the class and call on the people who usually knew the answers to recite. All of the papers that were supposedly done had the scores recorded in an old ledger on a day to day basis.

Once we had a neighborhood circus. We had tickets and a ticket window, tents made out of blankets and a center ring. I remember I was the fortune teller's assistant. I held a small metal shield that contained a deck of Old Maid cards that we told fortunes with.

I can also remember playing for hours on end under an old card table with a sheet draped around the sides. This was my castle on the long winter days, when it was too cold to go outside to play.

I remember as a little girl, taking several metal lawn chairs with my friends, and turning some over, and putting them into all kinds of different positions. Then we would get old blankets and cover the chairs, making a house. Our houses would always have several rooms, all designated of course. Once we had the house built, we were people on a desert or anything we wanted to be. But one thing outstanding in my mind, is how warm and safe we used to feel in those houses.

One student, early in the summer term, said that she had tried to straighten out her little sister on the matter of giants, instructing her that there *were* no such things. When she observed that this news had seemed more of a disappointment than a relief, I mumbled something about children knowing more of such matters than people suspect.

Some weeks later, this wise little note reached my desk:

> One other thing I wanted to tell you is you taught me some-
> thing super in class. I so often hope very hard for my little sisters
> to grow up right and good that I forget to let them be kids. The eight
> foot giant story—I know so well, because as a kid, I told stories of a
> reasonable facsimile and I even could take you to the place where
> my friend and I located his house on the same 4-H grounds. When I
> thought and thought about it, I began to see the importance in let-
> ting Carol believe and study her giant, just as I had done. In the end
> she will grow up to be a much finer person than if I stand by and say
> that I know it's not true because. . . . Because you know, there really
> *is* an eight foot giant that lives in the 4-H. He may be a few years
> older than when I knew him, but he still takes care of our neighbor-
> hood kids.

> As I have been observing children and really contemplating
> the significance of many of their actions, I have been reminded of
> my own experiences.

The backyard adjoining my own was neglected and had beautiful tall weeds—a perfect place for "War." A very old garage stood in the middle of it and had rotting boards and an upstairs compartment that was strictly "off limits." Great big P.O.W. letters were scratched on the walls by the older 11-year-old boys. I really didn't understand what the letters stood for, but the older boys knew, and when we were captured, we ended up there. Actually, it was sort of fun to be captured because we rarely had the chance to inspect the mysterious shack. An adjoining yard full of bumps and silky, long grass was the perfect place for running and jumping into foxholes. When I think back on it, it was amazing how many times we played war over and over again. Each time someone else was the enemy, the good guys, and the P.O.W.'s.

There are an endless number of games that children invent themselves. A favorite of my neighborhood when I was about 8 years old was "Horse and Stables." A line-up of all our bikes with spaces in-between were the stables. All but one person were horses and this extra was the trainer. He would take each of us out to train one at a time. We "horses" would run around the houses close by. Then, on our trainer's command, return to our own stable.

Every child should have a special hiding place. An old lilac bush in the neighbor's yard was my secret place. Inside the thin branches was a matted-down section just right for a very little house and a tea party—if there were not too many guests! The top of a tree made a very good place—especially when you could carve your initials on your very own branch!

Every Friday night all of my family would gather at my grandmother's house. My cousins and I were about 7 years old and decided to play "soda fountain" many of the times. My grandmother had a dishmaster, so her sink had more nozzles for us to use. Needless to say, we only had water, but drank it like chocolate milk. It's funny how we drank that water by the cupfuls, but if asked by our mothers to drink water—we'd find it a sickening job.

I remember running home from school to put on one of my mother's robes to play "nun" just like my teacher at school. The robes always worked very well until one of my friends' mother made her a real nun's costume. From then on, my nun games lost a bit of their flavor.

My brother was always the priest when we played. I must confess that I was jealous. It didn't seem fair that only boys got to be priests and altar boys. He said Mass and we sang the hymns we could remember from church. Our burial ceremonies fitted in well with this. The backyard was full of birds, turtles, cats, and fish. We made tiny crosses out of popsicle sticks to plant on the graves and could (of course) never step on the ground over our pets.

... About three years ago, a group of girls and I went to Lake Erie to go fishing. The fish were not biting and we found a piece of driftwood that looked like a conch from "Lord of the Flies." Without another word we began pretending that we were the deserted boys on a jungle island. We had the conch and the fire and the right atmosphere—the sand, "jungle," and water. I enjoyed myself very much and felt completely exhilarated after the experience.

I think the last incident shows that one does not outgrow his need for play and it thoroughly convinced me not to inhibit any playfulness that I feel.

To come to this realization is a sign of maturity. It is a relief to discover that the play spirit is intrinsic to human nature, that—universally potent and manifest in early life—it is yet not a "childish" thing, to be "put away," but a birthright to be treasured and drawn on throughout all of the years. Memory of your own play heritage is a way of keeping alive now all that you ever were while ripening into what you are yet to become.

....

CHAPTER TEN

Flying and Landing the Planes of Reality

> "Play is a voluntary activity or occupation executed within certain fixed limits of time and place according to rules freely accepted but absolutely binding, having its aim in itself and accompanied by a feeling of tension, joy, and the consciousness that it is 'different' from 'ordinary' life."
>
> Huizinga

A little boy who came into the restaurant turned around in his chair and slightly crouched down as though he was hiding behind a rock, and when I got close to him, pointing his fingers like a gun, made a sound like a machine gun. I turned around and looked; I had my hands full of plates. He said, "When you put those down, remember you're dead."

"The very existence of play continually confirms the supralogical nature of the human situation . . . " says Huizinga. "We play and know that we play, so we must be more than merely rational beings." "Notwithstanding the large affective cathexis of his play-world," Freud writes, "the child distinguishes it perfectly from reality." J. S. Bruner, in "Child's Play," reports:

> " . . . On closer inspection, it turns out that play is universally accompanied in subhuman primates by a recognizable form of 'meta-signalling,' a 'play face,' first carefully studied by the Dutch primatologist van Hooff. It signifies within the species the message, to use Gregory Bateson's phrase, 'this is play.' It is a powerful signal. . . "

The freedom with which children enter into and exit from the realm of play has already been illustrated in earlier evidence. They go from psychic sea-faring to palpable pie-eating and back in an instant.

Who can decide which, for a giant 747, is more amazing—taking wing to be borne by air, or rejoining the ground and coming safely to rest? A child moves between air and earth, mind and matter with wondrous ease (as a yearling baby—being closer to its base and resiliently flexible—falls down and bounces up again in a quality/quantity lost to bigger bodies). Children's skill in thus moving from one plane to another is clearly revealed in their low expectations of adult understanding of illusion ("in-play") and reality:

> While playing on the jungle gym one boy fell off. He was lying on the ground, very still; one of the teachers became worried and went over to him to ask if he was alright. His reply was "Sure I am alright—I am just playing dead, so leave me alone."

> One of the neighbors down the street from me had taken his two little daughters to a football game last fall (they were 3 and 4). This spring when they could go out and play they decided to play football. When I came by one was sitting on the front steps while the other was running to make a touchdown. I asked them if they didn't know that it takes two teams to play football. They replied, "Yes, we know, but it hurts too much."

> Girl (9) is leading pink-wigged dog (4-year-old boy) across stair landing. She calls to adults below, "See my pink poodle, Fifi." Fifi wags his behind enthusiastically, looking at his mistress from all fours. Adults say "That's a nice dog you have . . . etc." Fifi, in the midst of all the wiggling and waggling, suddenly lifts his head, pulls back the wig with one paw and says, "It's really me, Mama," and returns to being a dog in the same breath.

> Laura, a bright-eyed, happy 4-year-old, was swinging on the swing set in her backyard. Oblivious of what was going on around her, she was swinging as high as she could. After a few minutes, she slowed down gradually, stopped, and ran over to her tall, narrow, two-story playhouse.
> I followed her and asked if I could visit her house. She very graciously unlocked the door, and laughed when I bumped my head on the ceiling.
> She picked up her doll and began to fix her hair and clothes. She said this was her favorite doll, and that her name was Laura. She explained that the ribbon in Laura's hair was held on with a pin (first she called it a nail), but that Laura (the doll) didn't mind because that's the way it had to be held in. Very matter-of-fact. (I find it interesting that details like this are noticed by young children.)

She then placed the doll in her carriage and covered her entirely with blankets—"so she wouldn't get sunburned."

Laura showed me all her furniture—the kitchen table, the windows that really worked, the sink with faucet made of wood, and handles that turned. She said one side was hot water, the other cold. "It's not real water," she explained, "but that's alright."

She showed me the refrigerator and we talked about the "food"—various things painted onto the inside. I "took out" some frozen food and "ate it." But I was told quickly, "No, you have to cook it first!" (Of course, you fool, I thought. Nobody eats french fries without cooking them first!)

In Rackham the other day in *the primary class for mentally handicapped children,* it was news time. They reported seeing *Batman* on T.V. the night before (this is a frequent hot news item). The teacher expressed concern about what was happening in the story, and right away Darrel explained, "Oh, they're just acting. Don't worry! When they gas them and that stuff, they just use steam."

Last week I was again walking down the street after choir. I heard sounds as though someone was playing with a gun. I could hear the sounds of them cocking it and then shooting it. I kept searching to find out where the sounds were coming from. Finally on the left hand side of the street, I saw a little boy about 6 years of age standing by a third floor window and pretending that he was shooting at me. I decided that I would play the game with him. I waited until I was almost opposite him and then I said, "Oh! You got me." As I said this I slapped my hand to my heart and pretended to die. The little boy must have been quite shocked by the whole thing. He leaned out of the window and in a very pathetic tone said, "Did I really?"

(When a grown-up does suddenly play that well, it may at first surprise the child, who expected no response; it is difficult to be sure that adults know which world they are in!) One child, who had succeeded in drawing her mother into play (the mother agreed to address her as "Batgirl") found that some directing was required: "Say it better, Mom—with more expression!"

But the complexity of this mental marvel which enables human beings to probe questions of what is real must not be underestimated. The difficulty is evident in early childhood. Constant examination of inner and outer, mind and matter, visible and invisible is carried on:

> *Jennifer* (4): Mother, are we real?
> *Mother:*   Yes, Dear, we're real.
> *Jennifer:*   Oh! I thought we were play.

This is no simple matter. Are our dreams at night more or less "real" than our daytime acts—or differently real? Is the ghost in the closet—which must be exorcised before the child can sleep—real? In what ways is a person's name real? The desk is *really* made up of invisible, constantly-moving atoms; is its hardness and immobility, then, illusion or a different reality? Is the reflection in the looking glass real? It takes more time than all of humankind have had so far to figure out reality. No wonder each individual finds the quest a challenge:

> A 4-year-old, exploring the waiting room in a doctor's office, sees a partition between the patients and the nurses. He asks his 6-year-old brother, "Can you magic that away? Can you?"

> The child (2½) covered her eyes and then asked her sister, "Teedy, can you see me?"

> 2½-year-old girl, "I'M a wiggle worm." 3½-year-old girl, "You're not a wiggle worm, you look like it, but you're not, you're Rhonda."

> The 5-year-old who, when wearing her Halloween mask, kept asking, "Do you know me?" She thinks that the mask really changes her physically so that no one can recognize her. She's really comfortable being the wicked witch. The mask protects her from embarrassment.

The 20-year-old writing the above observation seems to have forgotten what the 5-year-old still remembers: the primitive potency of the mask, the ancient danger and grandeur of magic, the desire and fear of disappearing inside the transforming disguise. (The widespread adult custom of regarding children's minds as "little"—lesser—leads to a shrunken view of what transpires inside those minds, and to lost chances to learn from them.) "The 'differentness' and secrecy of play are most vividly expressed in 'dressing up,'" observes Huizinga:

> Here the "extra-ordinary" nature of play reaches perfection. The disguised or masked individual "plays" another part, another being. He *is* another being. The terrors of childhood, open-hearted gaity, mystic fantasy and sacred awe are all inextricably entangled in this strange business of masks and disguises.

The search for identity is a life-long quest in itself, and constant experiment is necessary in this process of discovery and development. Here are some characteristic examples of the role-changing in dramatic play so basic to this identity-exploring:

> My niece Stephanie provided me with a beautiful example of a child playing with others' identities. She is 3½.
>
> As I was sweeping out our tent she came in to watch. After asking several questions she finally said, "Ask me what's my name." When I inquired what her name was she replied, "Karen" (my name). I said, "Hello, Karen." She responded, "Hello. What's your name?" Joining in the game, I answered, "Judy." I was sure she wanted me to say Stephanie. She said with a protest in her voice, "No! *Stephie!* What is your name?" she repeated. This time I figured I had better answer, "Stephanie," if I didn't want to spoil the game. She replied with satisfaction, "Yes, Stephanie." She then picked up the sun glasses belonging to my husband. Putting them on, she inquired, "Now who am I?" I said, "Why Ron, how are you today?" "Fine," she said. Then she asked, "What's your name?" Of course I was now Karen again. Taking the glasses off and handing them to me, she asked, "What's your name with the glasses on?" "Ron," I replied. By this time the tent was finished, so the game ended.

> Keith (who just turned 6) asked, "What are you making?" I told him a poster and so he asked, "What's a poster?" I told him that a poster was a kind of sign you put up to tell people about something. He said, "Like not to play in an old mine?" I said, "Yes," then forgot about it. A little while later Keith and his brother Kevin (age 7) and their sister Karen (age 4) found a big box. Keith was a little boy lost in the mine. He crawled inside and they shut the top flaps over him. Kevin was his father, Karen his mother. Kevin: "Our little boy is trapped in this mine!" Karen: "Oh dear, Honey, what shall we do?" Kevin: "Don't worry, Honey, we'll get him out." He then called this same reassurance down to the little boy trapped in the mine. He danced around the box a little, tipped it over and hauled Keith out. Karen fluttered over him and asked him if he was all right. He lay there a while, then got up, announcing that now he would be the father and Kevin could be the son lost in the mine.

Perhaps another way of perceiving the child's ability to distinguish between play and "ordinary" life is through noticing what happens when the play-world dissolves, and the magic—the illusion—is broken (whether for a split second, for an hour, or for longer):

The two boys were already in the process of playing. From what I gathered, they were in a dungeon. One of the boys was a guard and the other was trapped; he was a prisoner. The prisoner was lying underneath the glass table. The guard was standing on one side of the "cell" (I heard them refer to it as that), at attention, one arm at his side and one arm bent as if carrying a rifle. "Please, let me out of here, I am going to die," the trapped boy said, his eyes pleading. He was really deeply involved in the part; I could tell by his facial expressions. The guard just said abruptly, "Shut up, I can't help you, you're just a prisoner." "Just let me have some water, something! I don't want to die." "You're gonna die anyway," the guard yelled, "because you are a murderer." I didn't catch this part of the conversation, but the prisoner grabbed the shoe of the guard and then the ankle, crawled out from under the table and pushed him, then said, "O.K., I got your gun." Apparently the guard didn't think so and shot the prisoner with his "gun." Before the prisoner had a chance to fire, he got mad and said, "I got your gun and I shot you first." They got into an argument about who killed who and they were very seriously upset about it. They both decided to stop playing because the prisoner was so mad he walked out of the house.

(Players: Kelly—3 and female, her brother Daren—5, Scotty—4, and his brother Brian, a very small 3)

Daren begins the play by telling Scotty, "You could be a cowboy." The two cowboys, Daren and Scotty, jump on their Hot Wheels. They carry their guns and drive fast and furiously up and down the sidewalk. Brian blocks the road for a moment with his hand over his mouth. He then hops on the grass and shoots a make-believe finger gun at passing Scotty, who returns a shot. Brian then darts to the house, then back down to the sidewalk.

Once again the Indian Brian blocks the sidewalk. Daren comes rapidly at him and Brian runs onto the grass, but is hotly pursued by Daren. Brian begins to cry, for Daren comes extremely close. As Daren gets off his "horse" and begins to tie a rope to it he says, "Indians don't cry!" He then hops on his Hot Wheel, shouts, "Let's go men! Stupid Indian!" Brian shouts, "I am not a stupid Indian!"

Kelly has dropped out of play. Brian moves to cover behind the tree near the sidewalk. As the cowboys go by, he darts out behind them. As he goes after one, the other comes to the rescue. The cowboys then have an argument with the Indian. The Indian attacks Scotty, who picks up his Hot Wheel and uses it as a guard.

The cowboys then run to the porch and return with long guns. Daren runs to his Hot Wheel, hops on and shouts, "Charge! I'm a tornado runningggggg!!!" The Indian takes an imaginary shot at the fleeing tornado.

Brian runs to the porch and gets the small gun and stands in the middle of the sidewalk. Cowboys come shooting and one shouts, "I'm missing him." Brian shoots. Daren shouts, "We don't get dead." Brian says, "I have a smoke gun." Daren: "I have a pollution gun." Scotty: "Pollution guns are the strongest!" "Smoke, smoke, I smoked 'im!" shouts Brian. The cowboy must feel smoked because he takes Brian's gun and returns it to the porch so "he won't kill us." Scotty: "Let him have it." Daren says no. Scotty then says he has to go home to eat his salad (figure that one out) . Daren is to guard the horses and guns. Brian gets on Scotty's horse and Daren raises the long gun as if to strike and orders him off. Brian gets off and Daren chases him home waving the long gun at him all the way. *End of Play.*

As the spring weather started to approach, baseball became a favorite game at recess. The third grade was out for recess and the boys were organizing a baseball game. One of the boys had ten men on his team and was arguing with the umpire that the extra boy should be allowed to play. The umpire suggested that he take the matter up with the captain of the other team. The two captains met at the pitchers' mound and after the first captain had presented his argument, the other captain stood and pondered the question. Finally, he said to the other boy, "I really can't help you sir, you'll have to take that matter to personnel." The other boy screwed up his face and very disgustedly said, "Really, John, that's the wrong game."

True play allows for no buck-passing, however witty. "Indeed," says Huizinga, "as soon as the rules are transgressed the whole play-world collapses. The game is over." If the Indian actually cries because he is afraid of being physically hurt; if the prisoner and the guard dissolve into impasse over who shot who first; if one baseball captain facetiously drops out of a sincere fight by wisecracking—then the strong yet fragile spell is broken. Most of the time, a child *can* tell the real players without a program.

"Into an imperfect world and into the confusion of life," Huizinga goes on, play "brings a temporary, a limited perfection . . . it creates order, *is* order." By thus playing with order and perfection in the other world of illusion, children practice accepting or changing the world that we call real.

···

CHAPTER ELEVEN

Playing with God

All One: Equality and Unity

"And the streets of the city shall be full of boys and girls playing in the streets thereof." *Zechariah,* viii, 5. Iona and Peter Opie found and have quoted this Biblical pronouncement in their fascinating *Children's Games In Street And Playground.* "Play is unrestricted," they write, " . . . play may . . . be the enactment of a dream . . . "

It is this freedom that seems to be at the center of play's immeasurable power. It is as unlimited in its range and potential as any human activity. It is both voluntary (nobody can force anybody else to play; the "suspension of disbelief" *must* be willing) and involuntary (it answers deep instinctual needs and erupts spontaneously according to its own inner laws). "The simplicity but yet the vastness of a child's imagination and concentration is astounding. Play is something you are, not something you do," writes a student.

Intrinsic to the freedom of the play-spirit is pure sincerity; playing cannot be faked. Probably the main reason why so many more young children know how to play so much better than most grown-ups is that life has not yet demanded that they learn insincerity; they have not yet begun to censor their own thoughts, feelings, actions. A baby riding in a grocery cart will regard the Queen of England and the carry-out boy with exactly equal candor, and he will stop paying attention to each at the very moment that his interest moves elsewhere. And if Mohammed, Moses, or Buddha appeared in the store aisle, all of them would be greeted with the same regard by that baby. A young child is not prejudiced for or against you by your doctorate, your empire, or your *Who's Who* listing. This superior innocence is fundamental to his freedom to wonder, and it is difficult to maintain under the duress of longer experience in this world. Consider this memorable scene in Shaw's *Pygmalion:*

Higgins:	. . . I can't change my nature; and I don't intend to change my manners. My manners are exactly the same as Colonel Pickering's.
Liza:	That's not true. He treats a flower girl as if she was a duchess.
Higgins:	And I treat a duchess as if she was a flower girl.
Liza:	I see. The same to everybody.
Higgins:	Just so. . . . The great secret, Eliza, is not having bad manners or good manners or any other particular sort of manners, but having the same manner for all human souls: in short, behaving as if you were in Heaven, where there are no third-class carriages, and one soul is as good as another.

Pygmalion-Higgins' irascible charm, his ability to "play" with language and with a transformation of street-vendor into duchess—are rooted in that freedom that he claims: to approach "all human souls" with equal honesty.

Children—for as long as they are still truly child-natured—go further; they extend the grace of their intimacy beyond the human. They are direct and unsentimental in all matters alike:

> Bryan came home from Sunday school and told his mother, "I tinkled in Jesus' bathroom."

Emerson would probably be pleased by such proof of his tenet that imagination functions to make us at home in new worlds, and by the casual hope of a hot-line evident in this next incident:

> My father was in a serious automobile accident at the beginning of the year. It was an accident that shook up our entire family, friends, and loved ones. . . . The week-end before last while babysitting for Keith (6-year-old) it came time to go to bed. It's customary for Keith to say his prayers with his mother or father, so I substituted. Keith remembered his parents in prayer, along with his friends, cousins, grandparents, the dog, me and my family, (each individually). When he came to my father, Keith glanced up at me and then back down to his folded hands. After he had said, "God bless Mr. Brown," there was a pause, and then he added, "By the way, God, how is Mr. Brown?"

> While babysitting I got Billy (5) ready for bed and asked him if he would say his prayers for me. He said he would and mumbled over some of the words and so I asked him "What was that last part?" He said, "It doesn't matter, prayers aren't in ENGLISH anyway."

I was teaching a unit on the earth and sky. This particular day we were going to have a lesson on gravity. Since I often underestimated the knowledge of these 6-year-olds, I was not at all sure how I should go about explaining this concept to the children. I decided to begin by asking the question, "Why don't we fall off the earth?", and see where we would go from there. I asked the question and got this answer: "God made the gravity."

Mom told me about one of the teachers in her school. She has a daughter about 3, Bethann, who she took to Sunday school the Sunday before Valentine's Day. The mother knew that they were going to discuss God and what He made: love. When the daughter came home, she and her mother made Valentines. She asked the little girl what they did in Sunday school. "Oh, nothing." So the mother asked what God made. "Nothing. He wasn't there," the little girl replied.

Which remark might mean not disillusion so much as the matter-of-fact expectation of seeing God when he does show up, wherever that may be?

Ann said, "God is everyone's Father. . .so God is really the Big Boss."

My daughter Tory, at age 4, meditating one night in the bathtub (a location conducive not only to dramatic but also to metaphysical play), roused herself from her thoughts to confer with me. "Now, how it is, is: I came out of *your* body, and you came out of *Grandma's* body, and *she* came out of *her* mama's body, and *she* came out of. . ." and she intoned this *Genesis*-like chant through several repeats before winding up the exposition: ". . .and it went back like that, a long and long time, till the beginning—but in the *very* beginning, out of whose body did *God* come?" I could only tell her the truth, of course—that nobody knows yet all about how the world and life began, but that people keep on trying to find out; that *she* might know more about it when grown up than I did. That answer was satisfactory to her for the moment—even promising—and for my part, I was pleased by the idea of being directly descended from God (whatever God's ancestry might be)! The Origins of Everything, the Ultimate Cause—there are no questions too big for children to ask. The most daring problems tackled by philosophers, scientists, artists (who dare because of their *own* childhood practice) may occur to a child between bath and bed. It is natural for them to seek connections between the familiar and the strange, the concrete and the abstract. Desire for knowledge is human. Curiosity—like fire and water—may sometimes be dangerous, but it is essential to life and learning. And a healthy child is quite at home asking high-powered questions of as high-powered an authority as the human mind can conceive or create.

These third-graders were responding to their Sunday school teacher's query: "If you could ask God a question, what would you ask?"

> I'd like to ask God what heaven is really like—is it like the U.S.?
> I would ask if the war in Viet Nam could end because so many people are being killed.
> Will I live forever?
> The question I would like to ask God is how many people are in the universe.
> I would ask God if everything in the Bible is true.
> The question I would ask God is Why did you make the other planets so far away?
> I would ask god if I cod have a dog.
> I do not no what I would say to God.
> If I could ask God one question. could I be better looking.
> What will my future be?
> I would ask him if he'd help us if in need.
> I would ask God if one of my puppies die, if he would have one waiting for me.
> Where do you live at?
> How did you make us?

Concise, no-nonsense requests for eternity, the heart's desire, and the secrets of creation. Children seem to find it easy to make primitive, poetic connections between known and unknown worlds:

> Two neighbor boys who had recently lost a grandfather by death were talking. The 6-year-old said he wondered how Grandpa could get to heaven. The 7-year-old said, "Haven't you ever looked down the railroad track? He climbs those stairs to the sky."

In this simple vision, earth fuses with air, physical transforms into psychic as inevitably as in the complexity of chemical or theological thought.

> It was snowing—the kind of snowfall where snowflakes fill the sky and seem to be everywhere. I plodded along in the snow about four paces behind a young couple and their little girl who was between 3 and 4 years old. She was the image of childhood, incapacitated by her hat, muffler, heavy snowsuit, boots, and mit-

tens. Mother was holding one hand and father was holding the other. As she shuffled along, she tipped her face toward the sky. She was giggling and giggling as she tried to keep her squinted eyes opened to observe the falling snow. As she went along, she carried on her own private conversation. "Stop it!" (a giggle) "Stop it!" (more giggling) "It tickles. God, you're tickling my nose."

So at the beginnings of life humans can play with anyone, anything, anywhere—for the pure joy of it—and can swing freely between the concrete and the abstract in a way that marks the highest forms of mature human thinking. "The world of the savage, the child, and the poet," concludes Huizinga, ". . . is the world of play." And those adults whose conscious and unconscious minds are still caught in the spell of this thing called play—who still remember those open secrets—can share, into any age, the vision of the growing child:

> "They see a whole new world opening before them—a world in which they will still be playing, but at far vaster games."
>
> Paul Hazard

Postscript

The very next day after this piece of work was "finished," a letter arrived from the University of York, England, written by my daughter Pamela (the one who—at an earlier age—taught me the lesson of "blessed receiving").

In a script almost indecipherable by all but dedicated readers (maybe Howard Johnson would heed such a "grown-up" handwriting), it contained treasure that came too late to be followed up and woven into this book, but was too rich to be left altogether out of it:

> . . . This will be a short letter, since it's morning and I *really* should be working and not writing letters at all...but I was looking through my notes yesterday, marking quotes for a paper I hope to start writing soon (cross fingers—it may be a potential chapter!) and I found some quotes on play which I realized that I'd copied more because they were relevant to your (our!) work than my (D. H. Lawrence) work, so I'll look them up and copy them for you. They're from an interesting book called *Life Against Death: The Psychoanalytic Meaning of History,* by *Norman O. Brown.* I thought you'd enjoy them. Here goes:
>
> > "This concept of childhood enables Freud to grasp a fundamental form of human activity in the world over and beyond the economic activity and struggle for existence dictated by the reality-principle. For children on the one hand pursue pleasure; on the other hand they are active; their pleasure is in the active life of the human body. Then what is the pattern for activity, free from work, the serious business of life, and the reality-principle, which is adumbrated in the life of children? The answer is that children play. . . .
> >
> > "Freud has thus put into his science the famous conclusion of Schiller's *Letters In The Aesthetic Education of Man:* 'Man only plays when in the full meaning of the word he is a man, and

he is only completely a man when he plays.' And from another point of view, Sartre says: 'As soon as a man apprehends himself as free and wishes to use his freedom . . . then his activity is play.'

". . . Boehme calls the perfect state 'play.' In 'play' life expresses itself in its fullness; therefore play as an end means that life itself has intrinsic value. . . .

". . . But from the Freudian point of view, every ordinary man has tasted the paradise of play in his own childhood. Underneath the habits of work in every man lies the immortal instinct for play. The foundation on which the man of the future will be built is already there, in the repressed unconscious; the foundation does not have to be created out of nothing, but recovered. Nature—or history—is not setting us a goal without endowing us with the equipment to reach it."

A hopeful note on which to end: the eternal evidence that there *is* no END . . .

A Selected Bibliography

Aristotle. *The Poetics.* Tr. Ingram Bywater. New York: Pocket Books, Inc., 1958. (Athens, 4th Century, B.C.)

Bett, Henry. *The Games of Children: Their Origin and History.* London: Methuen and Co., Ltd., 1929. (Now reissued by Singing Tree Press, Detroit, MI., 1968.)

Boyd, Neva Leona. *Play And Game Theory In Group Work.* Chicago: University of Illinois Office of Publications, 1971.

Britz-Crecelius, Heidi. *Children At Play: Preparation For Life.* Tr. Floris Books, Edinborough. New York: Inner Traditions International, Ltd., 1986 (first published in Germany in 1970).

Bronowski, Jacob. *The Origins of Knowledge and Imagination.* New Haven: Yale University Press, 1978.

Bruner, J. S., A. Jolly, and K. Sylva. *Play—Its Role In Development and Evolution.* Harmonsworth, Middlesex, England: Penguin Books, Ltd., 1976.

Courtney, Richard. *Play, Drama, and Thought: The Intellectual Background to Dramatic Education.* London: Cassell and Co., Ltd., 1968.

Douglas, Norman. *London Street Games.* London: Chatto and Windus, 1931. (Now reissued by Singing Tree Press, Detroit, MI, 1968.)

Erikson, Erik H. *Toys and Reasons: Stages In The Ritualization of Experience.* New York: W. W. Norton and Company, Inc., 1977.

Freud, Sigmund. *On Creativity and the Unconscious.* Tr. under the supervision of Joan Riviere. New York: Harper and Row, 1958. ("The Relation of The Poet To Daydreaming," quoted in Chapter II of this book, was written in 1908.)

Ghiselin, Brewster, ed. *The Creative Process: A Symposium.* New York: Mentor Books, New American Library of World Literature, Inc. (By Arrangement with University of California Press) 1955.

Giffin, Holly. "To Say And Not To Say: Skills of Dramatic Play." *Youth Theatre Journal,* vol. 5, no. 2 (1990), 14–20.

Gordon, William J. *Synectics: The Development of Creative Capacity.* New York: The Macmillan Company, 1968 (first copyright by author, 1961).

Hazard, Paul. *Books, Children and Men.* Boston: The Horn Book, Inc., 1944.

Huizenga, Johan. *Homo Ludens: A Study of the Play Element in Culture.* Boston: Beacon Press, 1950.

Koestler, Arthur. *The Act of Creation.* New York: The Macmillan Company, 1967.

Koste, V. Glasgow. "Meta-Thinking: Thoughts on Dramatic Thought." Paper presented at symposium ("Towards A Theory of Dramatic Intelligence: An Investigation Into The Nature and Origins of Dramatic Intelligence") at Harvard University. In Judith Kase-Polisini, ed. *Creative Drama In A Developmental Context.* Lanham, New York, London: University Press of America, 1985.

Opie, Iona and Peter. *Children's Games In Street and Playground.* Clarendon Press, 1969.

————*The Lore And Language of School Children.* London, Oxford, and New York: Oxford University Press, 1959.

Piaget, John. *Play, Dreams, And Imitation In Childhood.* Tr. C. Gattegno and R. M. Hodgson. New York: W. W. Norton and Company, 1962 (first translated into English in 1951).

Piers, Maria W. ed. *Play And Development: A Symposium* (with contributions by Erik H. Erikson, Jean Piaget, Konrad Lorenz and others). New York: W. W. Norton and Company, Inc., 1977.

Singer, Dorothy G. and Jerome L. *Partners In Play: A Step By Step Guide To Imaginative Play In Children.* New York: Harper and Row, 1977.

Sutton-Smith, Brian and Shirley. *How To Play With Your Children (And When Not To).* New York: Hawthorne Books, Inc., 1974.

Tolkien, J. R. R. "On Fairy Stories." *The Tolkien Reader.* New York: Ballantine Books, 1966.

Tolstoy, Leo N. *What Is Art?* Indianapolis and New York: Bobbs Merrill and Company, Inc., 1960. (First published in Russian, 1896.)

Torrance, E. P. and R. E. Myers. *Creative Learning and Teaching.* New York: Dodd, Mead, 1970.